Tayler Lewis

The Light by Which we See the Light

Or the Nature and the Scriptures

Tayler Lewis

The Light by Which we See the Light
Or the Nature and the Scriptures

ISBN/EAN: 9783337270544

Printed in Europe, USA, Canada, Australia, Japan

Cover: Foto ©Lupo / pixelio.de

More available books at **www.hansebooks.com**

THE VEDDER LECTURES. 1875.

"The Light by which we see Light,"

OR

NATURE AND THE SCRIPTURES.

A COURSE OF LECTURES

DELIVERED BEFORE

The Theological Seminary and Rutgers College,

NEW BRUNSWICK, NEW JERSEY.

BY

TAYLER LEWIS, LL.D., L.H.D.,

UNION COLLEGE.

'Ἐν ἀρχῇ ἦν ὁ λόγος.—John I. 1

NEW YORK:
BOARD OF PUBLICATION OF THE R. C. A.,
34 VESEY STREET.
1875.

WILLIAM FERRIS, Agent,
e Librarian of Congress, at

THE
VEDDER LECTURES.

1875.

PREFACE.

THE general title chosen for this little book is regarded as, more than any other, suggestive of its pervading thought. The study of nature alone is ever revealing more mysteries than it solves. At every step the darkness grows faster than the light. Endless links, endless adaptations, ever terminating in the physical—endless repetitions, in fact, of the same forms of force,—they never lead us out of the labyrinth, but only extend farther and farther, on every side, the limitless unknown. The soul cannot rest in this. It would know the meaning of nature. It earnestly asks: What is it all about? The inquiry itself is a religious one, and religion alone can furnish the answer. However dim or feeble this may be, it immediately elevates us above the depressing effects of mere physical knowledge. But religion without revelation, or faith in some kind of communion with the Infinite mind, is a shadow. Hence, the idea never lost sight of in these discourses: In Theology, in Christianity, in the Holy Scriptures, which we receive as the Word of God, there is a grandeur of thought unknown to any scheme of science, and which puts the humblest believer, however uncultured and unlearned, above the proudest intellect that is a stranger to any such influence. As Christians we should not hesitate to avow this, and firmly maintain it. We should appeal directly to Christian experience, as a *mighty fact* which science has no right to overlook. God's Word, if it be indeed God's Word, must be a λόγος ζῶν καὶ ἐνεργής, a "living power." It is not to be merely defended, or made the subject of tame apologies. It is to be carried with us, not as an obsolete relic, carefully enclosed in a guarded ark, but as our banner in front of the host. With this we conquer. Without it the most ingenious argumentation can only yield a seeming victory. "The Majesty and Glory of God beaming in the Scriptures," as some of our older divines were fond of calling it; this is to be our "Refuge and our Strength." As is said in the closing sentence of the Fifth Lecture: "The Bible itself must be brought out as the best defence against infidelity,—the Bible itself, not only as the great standing miracle of history, but as containing unearthly ideas for which no Philosophy, no Theory of Development, can ever account. To such study it will reveal itself as 'the Power (the δύναμις, or healing virtue) of God. Other defences are indeed important, but without this, they are shorn of the great strength which can alone make them available to the pulling down of strongholds and the overthrow of the truth's unwearied foes."

T. L.

SCHENECTADY, *June 4th*, 1875.

CONTENTS.

LECTURE I.
THE FEARFULNESS OF ATHEISM, - - - - 11

LECTURE II.
THE DENIAL OF THE SUPERNATURAL, - - - 57

LECTURE III.
THE COSMICAL ARGUMENT.—WORLDS IN SPACE, 103

LECTURE IV.
COSMICAL ARGUMENT CONTINUED.—WORLDS IN TIME, - - - - - - - - - - 141

LECTURE V.
THE KINGDOM OF GOD; OR, THE GREATNESS OF THE BIBLE THEISM, AS COMPARED WITH THE PHYSICAL, SCIENTIFIC, AND PHILOSOPHICAL, 187

LECTURE I.

THE FEARFULNESS OF ATHEISM.

LECTURE I.

THE FEARFULNESS OF ATHEISM.

The sharp issue—Moral dislike of the Thiestic idea on the part of some—Reluctance at wholly giving it up—Consequence of its abandonment, intellectual as well as moral desolation—The doctrines of hell and retribution less fearful—Chance and Law—Law as sequence merely—Atheism all horror—The seriousness of the world problem—The ideas of holiness and justice fascinating even in their condemnation—Atheism without hope, without *security*—Atheism may have its after state—The idea of progress has no foundation in such a view—Nature necessarily finite—Law of growth and decay—Cyclical movement—Retrogradations—Must run round and run out—Needs a renovating power—Plato and Aristotle—Argument for Diety must be something plain, adapted to all minds—Motion demands a Mover—Scientific cry: "Give it time enough"—On the Atheistic view the direction of the universal movement indeterminable. Illustrations—The Scientific Insect crawling amid the machinery of the great Harlaam organ; its mighty music all unknown—Higher aspects of the universe—The physical subordinate to the hyperphysical—Nature a *means*, has no *ends* terminating in itself—Mind, idea, first—The perfect, first—Melancholy view of Strauss—The despairing Prometheus.

IN a feature of the times which is most dreaded may be discovered one of the chief sources of hope for the cause of truth. We may reverently thank God that it is a day of sharp and inevitable issues. The most sacred truths, the foulest form of error, stand face to face. Difficulties in religion are weakened, or utterly vanish, when we see what immensely greater difficulties of irreligion our yielding to them must finally involve. Error must develop itself. It is a law of the thinking soul, as sure, as steady in its progress, as certain in its results, as any alleged evolution of the physical world. Error must develop itself. It is especially true of religious error. It has no tenacity, no holding-place. It cannot stand still; it must keep on, wandering farther and farther from the light, until it comes to that precipice of atheism beyond whose verge, or beneath whose verge, lies ὁ ζόφος τοῦ σκότους εἰς αἰῶνα, "the very blackness of darkness for ever." That issue is now presenting itself, short and sharp. The haze which has covered "the bridge of the war," as Homer calls it,—that has rendered indistinct and confused the middle ground of the battle-field—that has prevented our seeing truly the dividing lines of the opposing hosts—is fast clearing up. There is revealed a spectacle that, in one sense, may indeed be called appalling, and yet is full of encouragement in respect to the issue of the great conflict. Natural religion is gone; the old forms of deism have departed; difficulties of Scripture, questions of inspiration and canonicity are thrown into the background; pantheism has dropped its mask; apparent extremes have come together; a false spiritualism is found to be but a spectre of the grossest materialism. The mirage is dissolving; the ghosts have fled; and now there stand directly confronting each other, the two mighty foes that all along through all the illusions, and all the obscurities of the darkened battle-field, have been the only real antagonists. On the one side stands Christianity, the old Christianity, the only Christianity that has ever had power for the souls of men; on the other, blank atheism, with all the appalling desolation that connects itself with the thought of a godless world. As thus presented, we cannot doubt the final result. Our greatly disordered humanity is, indeed, full of paradoxes. The Apostle's charge is true. There is something in man's moral condition that makes painful the thought of a personal God when brought very nigh the soul. How to preserve something of the theistic idea, and yet avoid this disturbing moral consciousness, has been the problem ever since Adam "hid himself from the presence of the Lord God in the trees of the Garden." All history has shown how from this effort came nature-worship, pantheism, thence polytheism and foul idolatry. In this fallen and falling tendency, the divine idea is ever becoming more and more deformed on the one hand, or dimmed on the other,—ever more and more assimilated to ourselves in grossness, or philosophically refined away into an abstraction, an idea, a cause, a power, a bare force, divested, as far as possible, of all moral attributes.

And yet there is a struggle against its total

abandonment, when we are brought face to face with that sharp decision. When it nears that awful verge, humanity—the common humanity, as distinguished from that of the frigid speculatist, the common humanity, with its hopes and fears, its weariness and dissatisfaction—starts back with shuddering awe. It cannot take that last plunge, that reckless leap into total darkness. Religion cannot indeed be thought of by it without the accompaniment of fearful ideas; but here is something still more fearful. Much as it may have disliked the moral and retributive as inseparable from the personal aspect of the divine character, it cannot bear the thought of a universe without a creator, without a governing mind, without a providence, without a judge of right and wrong, making an eternal distinction between them, approving the one and condemning the other with an intensity to which the strongest human approval and condemnation can bear no comparison. It cannot part finally with the idea so deeply planted in the human soul, entering into all the mythologies, dramatically and epically represented in the world's highest ideals, that good must conquer evil, that right must triumph over wrong, that truth must prevail to the discomfiture of error, that there is to be an eschatology, whatever difficulties of place and time may be connected with such a thought—a latter-day development, somehow, and somewhere, that shall clear up the confusion and darkness that now cover the face of nature and the history of man. It may not logically reason out the position, but it feels unerringly that the total loss of the idea of God brings with it an effacement of all these distinctions. There is no virtue, no holiness, no right. There is no truth; it has no reality except as God's truth, as the emanation of an eternal mind, or its image as reflected in the finite comprehensions of the human soul. Facts may remain, or those sequences of facts which some call laws, but they represent nothing; they have no meaning, no *idea*. The intellectual universe is as truly gone as the moral. It is in the latter aspect, however, that the thought most readily comes home to us, and in all its withering desolation: The cosmos, like a vessel tossed in infinite space, driven we know not where on the currents of time, with no hand at the helm, no eye upon the compass, no course assigned or assignable, no reason conceivable why it should not ultimately drift in one direction as well as in another: Man, like a bubble appearing for a moment on the top of the nightly wave, mirroring for a moment the heaven of stars above, then vanishing into the void and formless deep. And then, too, there is the *terribleness* of nature, when there has wholly departed the belief in any power that can either protect us against it, or in any wisdom that can give us a reason, or furnish the ground of any conceivable reason, why we suffer from it, or why we should struggle with its irresistible forces. It is the thought of a universe without a guardian, without a Father, without anything to shield us from the direst woes that chance may bring, or a nature infinitesimally known in its parts, and utterly unknown in its great whole of power—a nature which we see to be full of the most awful catastrophes as they have appeared in the past, and which, for aught we know, may be immeasurably exceeded in the future. This may be called an overdrawn picture of gloom, but it hardly goes beyond that given by Strauss himself in his latest most melancholy book. It is true that, though having no better hope for himself than that of absorption into nature, he grasps at some idea of progress or order, tending to the good of the race or of the universe; but this, as we shall endeavor to show, he is compelled to borrow from another school, and his use of it is only evidence of his despair. Schopenhauer and Von Hartmann are more bold, or more unshrinking, in their conclusions. "Far better would it have been for this world," says the former, "if no living creature had ever dwelt upon it." "The universe," says Von Hartmann, "is miserable throughout." What a verification of the Apostle's language: ἄθεοι ἐν τῷ κόσμῳ—" Having no hope and without God in the world."

Men shrink from this when fairly seen in its awful desolation. The old religious fear is more tolerable. Hell becomes less horrible to the thought than such a hopeless atheism. There may be a reason for such an idea of fearful retribution, even if it be true, as some assert, that men have invented it for themselves. It is directly connected with the thought of moral distinctions, with their dread consequences when regarded as truly entering into the divine government. A personal God, not indifferent to right and wrong; if not *indifferent*, then making an infinite difference—approving the one and condemning the other with an intensity of interest as much greater than that of any human estimate as the ways of the infinite God are above those of all finite intelligences; there is reason in this, even as a possibility; and wherever reason enters, there is alleviation, something on which the soul can rest, finding, as it does, its own highest worth in such a moral destiny, even with all its alarming consequences. The thought of a personal God, not indifferent to sin—this once fixed in the mind and clearly held, the transition is direct to all the most startling verities of the Christian system. Retribution, atonement, grace, redemption, a great perdition, a great salvation, a great and divine Saviour, all become credible when there is truly realized the idea of sin. They all rise as it rises in the moral estimate, they all fall as it falls. When it goes out, they become incredible. Atheism, or what is morally equivalent to it, the rejection of the personal idea, is the ultimate antithesis of the old churchly belief, and one who commences the deviation should calmly estimate, in the start, the distance to which it must inevitably lead him.

To the mere scientist, or the mere speculative thinker of any class, atheism may not show its most frightful face. He is so taken up with himself, so intent upon regarding the universe as declaring the glory of the astronomer or the naturalist, that he has little or no thought for anything beyond. His eyes are holden from seeing that whatever belittles religion, belittles science and philosophy as well, rendering all human knowledge and all human aspiration as aimless and as valueless as it is ephemeral. His absorption in the physical blinds him to the true dignity of man as related to something above him, and transcending nature. In this state of mind, atheistic ideas may not distress him. So, too, the deep-seated, yet almost unconscious fear of a personal Deity may even awaken an instinctive feeling of relief in anything that veils it from the view. We are not afraid of Nature, terrible as she is, as long as the thought seems to screen us from a greater terror. There is a feeling that we can, somehow, take care of ourselves as against her. Her earthquakes, her pestilences, her upheavals, her terrific devastations, that have left such traces in the past, as they may come again in the future—all these carry with them no such dread, either in kind or degree, as that of falling into "the hands of the living God." And yet, with all this, there is an appalling hideousness in blank atheism when it fairly confronts our soberest thought. We cannot composedly resign ourselves to the notion of inevitable chance, introducing all conceivable forms and modes of being—all measure of possibilities being excluded by the absence of any ruling mind, and the consequent impossibility of conceiving any limitations to the rule of contingency. The survival of the strongest, even admitting that some such rule of forces might come in without the chance of reversal, may be the survival of the worst. The predominance of certain tendencies in the start must be wholly contingent, if it is wholly mindless, and that character cannot be lost in any subsequent movement. If it is chance in the beginning, it is chance throughout. As a whole, it might have been anything else, although in a tendency once originated, some partial movements may be controlled by others, and thus seem to have the appearance of means and ends. There is, indeed, an effort sometimes made to evade this. Chance is an odious term. The intellect, we may say, repels it, as well as the moral emotions. It is wholly idealess; it altogether eludes our thinking, unless we attempt to transform it in something else. It has been said, therefore, that chance is excluded by the idea of law, and that it is not so much in itself the antithesis of mind, as it is the opposite of method, order, recurring sequence. There has been lately a labored attempt to prove this; but those who assert it use words without meaning. Law as applied to nature, may indeed be said to be a figure: but is it not one to which we are forced if we would connect with our language any conceptions whatever? No more in the physical than in the moral and the political, can we separate law from the idea of a law-giver; and we must either wholly fall away from such idea, or we must trace it up, through man, through nature, to a pure personal mind. Without such a starting-point, the law itself, if we continue to call it so, the movement, the direction, in distinction from any other movement or direction, is a pure contingency. It is not difficult, we think, to detect the fallacy here. Had chance, among the infinite chances, produced any other state or system of things than that which now exists, it would, as far as we know, have been equally law, that is, equally entitled to that name as given to the sequence of facts. Had it been any other state of things, it would have had series of events capable of some kind of correlation. It would have had near sequences, remote sequences, intermediate sequences, hidden sequences, perhaps, we could not trace, and then they might have been called hidden laws received hypothetically, and afterwards verified, or modified, when there were discovered the intervening steps or links, as we would then call them. But these sequences, these connections with no other discoverable nexus than contiguity, might also have been something else, and no reason can be given why they would not, in that case also, have been *laws* as well as those that are found. Whatever *is*, is law, in whatever way events may follow. Law becomes sequence, and nothing more. We only cheat ourselves when we attempt to disguise it under another name. Every effort to get out of this utterly fails, until we connect them with mind, either near or remote, and then alone does this unthinkable conception of chance, τύχη, mere happening, cease to haunt our souls. On the materialistic hypothesis, the very ideas in our minds, through which we seem to recognize something more than sequence in events —such as the ideas of order, relation, causality— are themselves but products of this mindless, Godless power, and thus themselves as much contingencies as the outward sequences to which they are applied. Order might have been disorder if the atomic apparatus of our thinking had been so disposed. The positive philosophy, neither as first set forth by Comte, nor as delusively modified by Spencer and Mill, has any recognition of them as eternal and necessary ideas. And so, as between chance and mind, it has no right to recognize any intervening power. Law has really no place in such a scheme, except as the ghost of that divine idea which the atheistic materialist imagines he has slain.

There have been briefly stated some of the

things which may render atheism not only tolerable, but even desirable, for certain minds. But, after all, to the sober human thought it is an appalling conception, and men will not long remain under its gloomy shadow. When we are compelled to look the monster in the face, it is all horror. The sternest system of moral retribution ever connected with a theistic creed, challenges a preference. As has already been said, hell is less frightful than a Godless nature. There may be a reason for a condition of awful severity. It connects itself with the ideas of justice, of benevolence, of acting for a reason, and that reason the highest good of rational and moral being. We cannot bear to lose these ideas, though feeling that we take them at an awful risk. Our own reason and our own experience are sufficient to convince us of the possibility of something far beyond us here. It is not difficult for us to admit that our own moral state may be a fallen one, or such that we cannot estimate aright the heights and depths of the moral system of the universe. The human mind gets a glimpse of the idea that great glory, great exaltation, are connected with such a view, and that these are necessarily associated with the thought of great peril. Life thus viewed becomes a fearful thing. We tremble when we think in what an awfully serious world we live; and yet there is a fascination for the human mind, even for the depraved human mind, in the idea of an infinite justice and an infinite holiness, though involving the thought of infinite severity towards the unholy and the unjust. Commensurate with it is that other idea of infinite goodness which the rational soul affirms as a necessary attribute in the conception of Deity, even though the sense-evidence of its manifestation may be overpowered by an immense balance of seeming evil in the world in which we dwell, or even did we find ourselves in a department of the universe where nothing could be discerned but unalleviated and uncompensated woe. There is something sublimely terrible to man in the idea of this perfect divine holiness. It so condemns us, whilst giving such an awful dignity to our being in its moral relations to such an attribute. It transcends all other moral ascriptions. The Holy One! There is no language of the Bible, no epithet of Deity that has such an awe for us. And yet, as I have said, it has a fascination for the contemplative spirit, even when deeply conscious of its own unholiness. The thought is perfectly conceivable: a human soul, fearful in respect to its own moral condition, trembling even under the dread of condemnation, yet preferring this personal risk to the utter loss of that glorious conception of the ineffable righteousness, so grand even for the intellect, could we separate it from the moral emotion. The "correlation of forces," the highest power the materialist admits! How it pales before the sublimity of this theistic language: "The Righteous Governor of the Universe." The Holy One "in whose sight even the heavens are not pure." There is, indeed, a fearfulness in the theistic thought, an awe even in its aspect of beneficence; but it is, at the same time, the ground of all hope, as it is of all human dignity. We cannot do without it. We cannot lower it, though it so condemns us.

But atheism is without hope, without glory, as it is without reason. It has its own terrors, with nothing to calm them. It gives the soul no security against the direst conceivable evils, whilst it takes away every moral ground or reason for believing in any ultimate triumph of truth and goodness. Such a hope illumines the darkest aspect of theism: "Clouds and darkness are round about God, but righteousness and judgment are the foundation of His throne." There is a reason for everything. In the godless view there is a reason for nothing. Every destructive movement is conceivable, possible, and even probable,—only give it time enough, as a class of scientists are so fond of saying. There may be retrogradations, deteriorations,—if we may use such words where there is no standard according to which they may be reckoned, no hyperphysical measure by which they may be determined. There may be a progress, seemingly such, yet only a progress in horror. There is no security, even, against the direst forms of evil that are feared or fancied as connected with the religious view itself. This awful, unknown nature may have its devil and its hell. As it has produced monsters in the past, so may it continue to produce monsters in the future. It may supersede man by the evolution of a new race, transcending in depravity, as it transcends in strength and demonic sagacity, the one that for six thousand years—twenty thousand, say some —has made this world a Golgotha of crime and misery. If we follow on the analogy, we cannot refuse to admit that there may be evolved a state of things which shall throw into the shade the enormities of all preceding periods. Take away the ideas for which we are indebted to religion and revelation; view man simply as a product of nature, with no other hopes than nature gives, and we are safe in saying that no one of the geological ages has surpassed in destructive enormity, in irrational waste of life, the human cycle. Had we remained gorillas, the earth would not have been so filled with blood— with crimes against nature exceeding in horror all actions that beasts could commit. My hearers will not mistake me here, nor misunderstand the hypothesis of total and hopeless irreligion on which such statements of human facts and human possibilities are grounded. We may take a step beyond this. Paradoxical as the language seems, nature may produce a false God. Give it time enough and there may come out of the physical evolutions some dire consciousness, corresponding to that awful being whom the infidel imagination gives us in its deformed caricature of the Scriptural Deity—a power vast, malignant, irresistible, having in it the concentrated evil drawn from all the productive forces of the universe. Given a past eternity for nature's working, she may have long since produced such a being, having his seat of power somewhere in the infinite space, and extending to remotest distances his malignant rule. And so, too, in regard to another life, another state of being for man. Irreligion sometimes boasts that she has slain that chimera of superstition. Man may now eat and drink without that haunting fear of something after death. But neither for this does atheism give security. The human protoplasm may live on, carrying with it the human consciousness, the human identity. It is one of the forces of the universe, and may preserve its individuality in other conditions, or as correlated to other forces. Science can give no security against this, or against any evils its changed physical condition may involve. It may still be true that the conscious sensualist "lifts up his eyes, being in torment"—the torment of an unknown physical hell.

Or we may take another view coming out of that doctrine of atoms to which atheism has run for shelter since the days of Democritus. Although the microscope has never made an approach to this mysterious domain, never having brought to light an atom, or a molecule, or even a molecular combination, yet here, in this utterly unknown region, a certain kind of science finds life, consciousness, memory, thought, imagination, reason, will—all that constitutes personality or individuality in our present state of being. We are what the atoms make us, nothing more. And this, too, their making, resolves itself into site, number, relation—in a word, arrangement of constituent atomic points. We can conceive of nothing else; and here the thinking of the common mind is as clear and trustworthy as that of the most scientific, since to both this atomic world is alike unknown. All that we can say is that the doctrine gives no security against that dreaded idea that man may live again—may live in pain, in agonies inconceivable. Take time enough, and apply to it the mathematical doctrine of chances, there arises not merely a possibility, but a high probability, growing evermore nearer to an absolute certainty, if this atomic hypothesis of the origin of life have any truth. Of any individual man now existing it says that his spiritual powers are but the results of such or such a combination of these elements of all being. They make him *what he is*, and he has no other being. From them come not only his flowing body, but his thought, mind, will, consciousness—yea, even what he calls his reason, though that, too, is only position, arrangement, number, as much as his sense or his very flesh. Now, in the infinite tide of surging material being, these atoms, or precisely similar atoms, may come together again. It is extremely probable, on the doctrine of chances, that they *will* come together again—the *when* or the *where* in no way affecting the estimate or the identity of the being. They come together just as they were, whether a moment before, or at a time which the longest decimal notation fails to estimate—they come together at last, and there he is again, the same consciousness, the same memory, or, so far as these constitute identity (and we cannot conceive of it separate from them), the same identical being, carrying with him all the misery of his former existence, enhanced by the absence of all security against ten thousand fold greater misery in the future. There is no hand at the helm of the universe, and there is no telling, no conceiving the horrors into which it may drift.

But there is the idea of progress, say some—progress continually tending towards a better state, towards a higher order, a higher happiness, a higher intelligence—in a word, a higher good. Some such dream meets us, now and then, in the writings of Herbert Spencer. But what is meant here by higher and lower? To determine this, in respect to any movement, we want a standard, a rule, a direction, out of and higher than such movement. If there is nothing transcending nature, nothing outside of nature, nothing for which nature itself exists, how then are we to measure it, or ascertain its tendencies? We are in the balloon; no star above is seen; how know we whither it is going? We have no sighting point for our survey. Progress towards what? This must always remain the question. And then, even if we *can* get a measure, or fix a direction, what assurance against retrogradations or deteriorations? Everything in the smaller nature, or natures, that fall under the eye of our science, presents the turning or cyclical aspect. Birth, growth, decay, death, dissolution, we can conceive a reason for them as explained by the relation of things to a sphere above nature; we can believe that they have a counter-acter, or a regulator, or a compensation, or some clearly-explained end in some higher system of ideas. Without this, however, there is no resisting the analogy that drives us on to extend this law of growth and decay, of cyclical change, to the universal nature as well as to the smaller natures that always exhibit it as far as our induction extends. The whole cosmos may wax old and decay. Scientists were once puzzled with the apparent anomalies of the solar system, such as change in aphelion and perihelion, shortening of orbits in one direction, undue lengthening of them in another, all indications of disorder that might terminate in remediless decay and final ruin. La Place, it is said, showed the contrary of this—that is, he proved the perpetual stability of the solar system. Apparent disorders had their maxima and minima, and thus the great order would go on for ever. But, admitting that he had shown this, or something like it, in regard to the solar system as a thing by itself, separated from the universal cosmos, and having its own correlation of forces—admitting that all its apparent irregularities were counteracting checks to each other, so that none of its members would, by means of them, ever get too far from the sun, and thus be thrown off as wanderers in space, or too near, and thus be drawn into the vortex of its consuming fires—admitting all this, we say, his purely mathematical argument, though holding true of the data immediately before him, did not take into account other disorders, other decays, other redundancies, other retrogressions that might have their causal force in the internal constitution of each member. According to the present nebular and ring hypothesis, they had been for countless ages throwing off their heat, radiating into infinite space, cooling, condensing, diminishing in magnitude, increasing in density, changing their relative distances and attractions. The great central body had, during the same countless ages, been undergoing incalculable transformations. It was, therefore, an argument purely mathematical, purely hypothetical, based on assumed magnitudes, masses, densities, and mean distances, as they are now seen, or supposed to be. It did not take into account—it could not take into account—other disordering influences that might come from the unnumbered bodies floating in infinite space outside the solar system. It overlooked the vaster revolutions and evolutions in which our system and our earth must participate, however slow the changes that might thereby be produced in the relations of its parts, or however imperceptible the motions determinative, at any time, of its own absolute place in the universe. These are views to which the most modern observation is now forcing us. If trustworthy, they give us a glimpse of an immeasurable unknown, in relation to which our science, now so greatly lauded, is truly a smaller thing than was the knowledge of Ptolemy, as compared with that which was revealed in the first discoveries of the telescope. The ancient centre is again unsettled, but the true centre is as far as ever from being fixed. As thus compared, infinitesimal is the enlargement of our knowledge, infinitesimal is any fancied increase in the value of our cosmical speculations. One word, one promise, one whispered hope that we can believe in as coming to us from the Infinite Father, is more than worth it all. We have learned distances, motions,—we have a dream of correlated forces; that is the sum of our attainment. It is almost wholly mathematical. La Place, with his Mechanique Celeste, is as small here as Hipparchus. In one sense he is far behind Pythagoras with his sublime imagination of the " music of the spheres."

But waiving all that as utterly beyond our reach, let us proceed to other and more general considerations. We remember how this view of La Place in respect to the stability of the solar system was hailed by the Christian world. It was, however, on the ground of its furnishing, or its being supposed to furnish, to those who needed it, an argument for a divine idea, a divine care, in the originating and in the adjustment of our solar system. It was the work of the great geometrician, as Socrates styles him. Not so La Place himself. He may have smilingly accepted the gratitude of the pleased religionist, but he saw no hand of God in the cosmos. The heavens told the glory of the French astronomer, not of the Great Architect above. Their interest lay in furnishing the diagram, the black-board, as we may style it, for his mathematical speculations. They were filled only with sines and cosines, tangents, differentials, integrals, infinite series, relations simply of number, figure, distance, motion, space; empty of all else. To him this principle of counteracting order, of assumed stability, belonged to nature itself; and that was something he could never prove. An inherent power of recovery, or of rising from a really lower to a really higher state, an inherent rectification of a real disorder, without aid from a plane above the natural—such a property as this no science could ever demonstrate. The mightiest application of the calculus fails here. Mathematical theory and induction are both unable to show that any great section of nature, much less the great whole of nature, is exempt from the principle of growth, maximum, decay—in a word, of a necessary finiteness, which the smaller inductions have invariably proved to belong to every partial nature, from the plant to the growing, decaying, and disruptured planet. The condition of growth seems to necessitate that of decay. The force required to keep an organism at its maximum must be greater than that required to reach it; since all beyond must be an addition, a coming of more from less, which is the same with something from nothing. The coiled spring must first relax its tension, and then return with more or less rapidity in its recoil to its former state. So that which has no other origin than a nebula in its lowest state of material existence, and no other law of its being than the condensation, or the unwinding of that nebula, whichever view we take, forbids the idea of eternal progress, or of unchanging movement in either direction. It must have its cycle, returning through all changes, either to perish, or to make again the same revolution, thus accomplishing a cycle of cycles, in which each maximum is continually less than the preceding, until it goes out, or is lost, or assumes some new form in the great whole of forces, therein to repeat a series of similar perishing revolutions. Whatever grows may decay—must decay. So induction teaches, if it is to be our only guide. Now it is a peculiar feature of the modern scientific infidelity, that it assumes this of the universe. The cosmos *grows* as well as the fungus. Solar systems, stellar systems, all came out of that lowest state called the nebula. Science can show no leap in the process of growth and decay, no point where perpetuity necessarily comes in, or the analogy permits us to stop short of the idea that there is in nature, even as a whole, a necessary finiteness of force, however vast the extent of space through which its manifestations may be dispersed. It must run round, and finally run out, whether to come up again, or come out again, as the old Stoics maintained in their doctrine of rarefactions, or to be no more for ever. The necessarily infinite alone remaineth *ad eternum*, whilst all things below the infinite must have the measure and the uses that it appointeth to them. " The grass withereth, the flower fadeth," nature comes and goes, but "the Word of the Lord abideth for ever." All that is not God is necessarily finite, except as He sustains, restores, perpetuates.

The reasoning of Plato here, and to some extent of Aristotle, can never be refuted. I refer to the great argument of the latter philosopher by which he proves the necessity of the ἀκίνητος, the Immovable, as a principle lying above motion and the movable; in other words, an infinite mind, an eternal thought, as the only ground of stability in the universe. So Plato shows that the existence of antagonisms, or the generation of opposites, or correlations of forces in nature, must come from something above the plane of the physical. For although such seeming equilibriums may be produced, as it were, by partial currents, or counteracting eddies, in the same movement, yet nature *as a whole* can never of herself generate a direction above that, or the opposite of that, in which she is tending, and which, unless counteracted or regulated by a power from without, must inevitably bring her to a suicidal end. It is idle to say that these men, great thinkers as they were, had not science enough to warrant them in making such declarations. The whole question lies above any sphere of science, or fact induction, even were not the comparative difference here between the ancient and modern knowledge the infinitesimal we have shown it to be. The illustrations, too, presented by these old authorities, are as good as any that are furnished by the vocabulary of our modern progress. If *genesis*, development, says Plato, or what we call evolution, or progressive movement, were ever εὐθεῖα, straight onwards, in one direction, it must finally tend to extinction. Whatever the principle, be it rarefaction or condensation, separation or combination, cold or heat, cooling or heating, it must, in the one case, reach a state where all cohesion, all organization ceases, or, in the other, come to a stand in which all life, all motion, terminates in absolute immobility. Or, to use his own most expressive language, " things would cease *becoming* and genesis would be at an end." In more modern terms, the correlation of forces, if given an eternity to work in, would at last produce an absolute equilibrium, a state of *rest* which is the maximum of force, even as motion, on the other hand, or regarded as a departure from this state, is ever a spending or letting out of force, and must terminate in the absolute nothingness of inertia. Hence, that the cosmos may live, says the philosopher, there must be at some point or points, a καμπή, or *turning* round, a deviation from the progress or tendency in which it is going, a change from one law or from one movement to another, and this can be no product of that law, or that movement, from which it is turned. There may be such a seeming law of cyclicity, or self-regulating cyclical return, in the partial natures; but in them it must come from other partial natures without, which, at certain points, connect with and counteract, thus causing partial deviations. As applied, however, to a nature regarded as universal, and *having nothing outside of it*, this idea, of course, cannot be admitted. There, the result of such a right onward movement is demonstratively inevitable. Nothing can save from it but the supposition of dynamical laws, that is, principles of motion and force, utterly different from those our best science acknowledges in physical and cosmical investigations. Gravitation must destroy itself, if there be no principle, higher, remoter, stronger, in the universe.

The perverseness of an atheistic science may drive us to a mode of argument that seems labored and abstract; but it is in order to meet this perverseness on its own ground. The truth must be something more simple than this— something which the common, healthy mind perceives, as well as the most reflective and logical. It cannot be that God, who made the human intellect, could have intended that the proof of His own existence, of His own intellect, we may say, should be so difficult, or so little obvious, as to allow the soul to have, even for a moment, an excuse for its scepticism. We should never depart from the intuitive idea that in motion, in change of any kind, in the least phenomenal deviation of anything (whether whole or part) from a former state, there is evidence of will somewhere in space and time, of a purpose and a volition without which such deviation never would have been, however many, or however undiscoverable, the connecting links of causation. We should hold to this as a proof preceding any that we draw from the more recondite field of organic life. In truth, once admit motion, self-motion, to be a property of matter, and it is not easy to deny that life also may be such. It is not easy to distinguish between life and self-motion. Hence Aristotle, in the argument referred to, begins at the beginning. Motion demands a mover, and that ultimately a prime mover, itself unmoved and immovable, or a will originating motion, itself outside of any moving chain of cause and effect. In the same way the argument of Socrates against the atheists in the Tenth book of the Laws. Motion is proof of soul. In an afterstate, clearer perhaps intellectually, because purer morally, we may wonder at ourselves for ever allowing this intuition to be obscured. Then may we feel, as we have never felt before, the reasonableness of that chiding, though gentle remonstrance : " O ye of little faith, wherefore *did* you doubt?"

The sceptical scientists are very fond of drawing on time. If any form of "evolution" be insisted on, or of "natural selection," or any adjustment of atoms driven by chance, and after infinite misses and infinite incongruities falling, at last, into something to which we give the name of order—the demand is ever for time, more time. If we do not see species coming out of species, or any of the half-way transition processes, then science becomes humble again; we are reminded of the limited observations necessarily inadequate for such a vast induction. Only grant time enough, and we can prove the possible happening of anything conceivable. Now this accommodating demand may be turned the other way, and to the confusion of those who are most fond of making it. They would keep it within some bounds of the decimal notation. Billions, trillions, decillions, might, perhaps, satisfy their very modest hypotheses. But as against them, we may draw at once on the bank of eternity. How long before we reach it, or even make an approach to it, ought an infinite, ever right-onward moving nature to have passed over the *finite*, the very finite, progress to which we see she has now arrived. Or, whatever may be the direction she is taking, at what an ancient time in the long-past eternity, must she have to come to its ultimatum, if there be no hand to make the *turn* of which Socrates speaks. How many ages ago must there have been reached the immovable equilibrium or the irrecoverable dispersion? An eternity before our day must this binding or loosing—for motion is ever the spending of force—have brought all things to their maximum of solidity or their minimum of rarefaction; in both of which states all life perishes, all motion and resistance as the very conditions of manifested sentient being. The machine has run down, or run out. It is a consequence of that finiteness which necessarily belongs to everything moving in time and space. At such a juncture, the Platonic myth in the Politicus supposes the hand of Deity again to take the helm. On the hypothesis that excludes such a controlling and restoring idea, nature, or the physical universe, has come to a dead-lock from which there is no renewal. If we take it in one direction, the result, as has been already said, is a balance of forces, a static equilibrium of *resistance*, which is only another name for absolute *rest*. If we follow it in the other, the only idea left is that of utter dispersion, which is only another form of absolute inertia. Thus are we driven to the thought of a power outside of and above nature, a power demanded for its conservation and restoration as much as for its primal origin. "Of old hast thou founded the earth; the heavens are the work of Thy hands. They perish, but Thou remainest. As a garment do they wear out; Thou renewest them, and they are renewed. But Thou art HE (the same), and of Thy times there is no end."

But, aside from any such reasoning, the doctrine of progress, in which the atheistic scientist takes refuge to escape the horror of his own conclusions, or this tendency to a higher and better state which Matthew Arnold describes as "a making for righteousness," is all a sheer assumption. How do they know *whither* nature, the universal nature, is going, or whether it be *up* or *down?* Certainly not from any induction. The atheist, or scientific atheist, is very fond of talking of the vast extent of the cosmos; he very confidently compares his own views in this respect with what he deems the religious narrowness; but as related to the whole, of which he so presumptiously judges, what is the mighty difference between his knowledge of the universe, as taken in all directions, and that of the most ignorant religionist of ancient or modern times? We speak, of course, comparatively. Franklin's wise ephemeron, drawing his inferences as to all surrounding being from the vernal or autumnal changes in the leaf on which he sits, would present the most apt illustration of this folly. Or we may imagine the tiny insect crawling in the great Haarlem organ. He may be a most scientific insect, possessing the keenest sense, endowed with a vision surpassing all the powers of the microscope. There is nothing in his minuteness at war with the supposition of his having a most mathematical brain, which nature, or the collocation of the atoms, or some nice adjustment in the correlation of his vital forces, may have bountifully given to him. There he sits, with all the materials for a Mechanique Celeste in the smaller, that La Place possessed for the supposed wider sphere. He is intent on the study of strings and pipes, and the most minute adaptations of the mighty apparatus, so far as his angle of vision can take in an almost infinitesimal part. He sees the valves open and shut; he traces, for an inch or two, the cords by which these effects seem produced; he begins to classify them and to talk of laws, thus turning phenomena into forces, and dignifying mere sequences with the name of causes. His induction may rise to the conception of mightier pipes, of more distant keys, of deeper valves, of hidden strings; but he never in this way gets out of the machine. It is, all through, as far as he can see, adaptation for the sake of adaptation, evolution for the sake of evolution. But what is it all about? Sometimes, as Tyndall occasionally confesses, he may have his hour of weakness. Now and then his cerebral organization may become strangely impressed with the idea of something haunting the machinery, or that there is "a spirit in the wheels" —a blowing, or breathing in the pipes, which none of the sense-causalties before him can explain. There comes the faint consciousness of some vibrating tremor in the vast surrounding apparatus. It startles him with the idea of something greater than he sees. It may be the hope of a grander being, or a sense of danger filling him with alarm. There is something more serious in the machine than he had imagined. Is it a dream—a dream that he is dreaming, it may be—and from which he shall awake to a higher consciousness? There may come, as from a far distance, the faint sound of a mighty music, of a glorious anthem rolling above. Or there may arise in his insect soul, or in some way be given to it, the idea of a higher world, a more real world, to which this intricate valvular apparatus may be subservient, and from which it derives all its value. But this he soon dismisses as utterly unscientific. He returns again to "common sense," to confidence in his sharp eye, his groping touch. " The things that are seen ;" they are the only realities after all. " The things unseen " —all that is supersensual—they belong to the world of phantoms which experimental science —the only science—can never admit.

The illustration is a fair one. From induction alone it is impossible to determine whether this physical apparatus in which we are involved, out of which we are evolved, and into which our *seeming* individuality is soon to be resolved again, is really tending to order or disorder, or towards anything we might indulge our fancy in calling *higher* or *lower* states of being. The very terms point to something out of the physical, above the physical—something which measures nature, but can never be measured by it.

Such a comparison is unimpeachable as long as we take for its basis any conceivable ratio between the infinitesimally known and the infinite unknown. To vary the illustration, however, let us suppose an almost invisible insect crawling upon the dome of St. Peter's. He possesses a sense of vision keener than the human. His microscopic eye does, indeed, see chasms, and roughnesses, and inequalities, which may disappear to a survey made from a higher standpoint; but what does it tell him of the purpose for which that vast structure was reared? What does it tell him of its transcending spiritual significance? Or, to confine the thought to what might be deemed, in strictness, the more proper scientific field, what does it tell him even of the space or mathematical direction of his seeming progress, or whether he is moving on a surface ascending or descending, concave or convex, or whether, taken as a whole, it may be called plane or spherical, or at what rate the vast arc, to which his short vision can draw no tangential line, may be changing its mighty curvature.

Equally preposterous is the claim that is made to determine, by any scientific induction, the movement and direction of the cosmos in any higher aspect that we may call spiritual, moral, metaphysical, ideal—or even in that lower view which excludes all but the physical as exhibited solely in the phenomena of motion and force. Even if the things immediately around us presented no anomalies or unevennesses, no apparent retrogressions or deteriorations, what help do our second of time and our inch of space give us towards determining any present state, or future tendencies, or final evolution, of that great whole of being of which we form, physically, so insignificant a part? The believer may legitimately connect such an idea of progress with that of a physical world subordinate to a moral probation, and the theatre, ultimately, of a high moral production. This is in true harmony with the thought of the cosmos as the work, through whatever process of origination and continuance, of a personal Deity, infinitely strong, infinitely wise, infinitely just and good. It matters not whether we say this comes from revelation, or has some claim to be regarded as an *a priori* idea of the human soul, or whether we regard both these supposed sources as substantially the same. If the latter, or the *a priori* view is preferred, it would denote simply something mirrored in the finite from the infinite mind, or a reflection from that image of God of which the Scriptures speak. On either view, naturalistic, theological, or metaphysical, thought, ideas, are *a priori* somehow, and somewhere. One position is that they existed in a necessary, an eternal, and an infinite mind, before they came into the human, carrying with them some recognizing glimpse of their necessity and infinity. The other likewise necessitates what may be called an *a priori* being, but of an infinitely lower kind. It would consist in those arrangements of atoms, and those correlations of forces, which, when brought out in the lucky confluences of immeasurable time, might constitute the individual man. We all had our primeval being in the nebula; we were all born out of it, as it will be to all of us the grave of our existence. But with *a priori* or necessary ideas in any other sense, the positivist has nothing to do. He denies their existence. He assigns them to the chimaera region of metaphysics and theology. He goes by experiment, in a word, by sense, acknowledging no higher source for any human thought. When he talks, therefore, of progress, as Spencer is compelled to do, or of an inherent "tendency that makes for righteousness," to use some of Mathew Arnold's favorite lingo, he goes entirely out of the sphere to which the fundamentals of his philosophy necessarily limit all human knowledge. He is trespassing on another province of which, at other times he affects to speak with contempt.

It would have been more wise, it may be thought, to have taken for the subject of this lecture a nearer and more threatening form of infidelity. But atheism is the goal to which it all is running, even as all irreligion is a dislike to the idea of a personal God. We may rejoice, however, that it carries its antidote along with it. There is nothing, perhaps, that will ultimately better subserve the cause of religious belief than the last published work of Strauss. After reiterated denials, and long struggles with the vortex into which he saw himself irresistibly drawn, it is pure atheism at last—blank, unqualified atheism. The English scientific sceptics seem drawing back, but Strauss has pushed on to the ultimatum, and it stands before us in all its horrors. Nothing that I have said of the awful desolation of a soul that comes fairly to see what it is to be "without hope and without God in the world," presents such an appalling picture as he himself has given us after announcing his utter loss of faith in God. All his philosophy, all his logic, all his scholarship, yield their latest fruit, their only fruit, in such an utterance as this: " In the enormous machine of the universe, amid the incessant whirl and hiss of its jagged iron wheels —amid the deafening crash of its ponderous stamps and hammers—in the midst of this terrific commotion, man, a helpless and defenseless creature, finds himself placed—not secure for a moment, that on some unguarded motion, a wheel may not seize and rend him, or a hammer crush him to powder. This sense of abandonment is at first something awful." Yes, we may say, not only at first, but evermore, the more it is contemplated, growing denser in its gloom, more suggestive of that fearful language of the Scripture, "the blackness of darkness forever." In other places Strauss would modify the horror of such a view by throwing himself upon some of those *a priori* ideas of ultimate order, to which, as we have seen, he and his confréres have no right. But in this terrific passage, he reminds us of that wild, despairing farewell to nature, which the prince of Grecian dramatists puts into the mouth of the Jove-defying Titan, as amidst storm and earthquake he goes down into the unfathomable subterranean deeps:

> ὦ μητρὸς ἐμῆς σέβας, ὦ πάντων
> αἰθὴρ κοινὸν φάος ἑλίσσων,
> ἐσορᾶς μ' ὡς ἔκδικα πάσχω.
>
> O thou, my awful mother earth, and thou,
> Aetherial sphere unrolling evermore
> The common light! Behold ye my dark doom?

There is no escape from the terrible machinery which Strauss so vividly depicts, and all the horrors it involves—these horrors, too, made immensely greater for man from the fact that he has the Promethean fire of reason to contemplate his inevitable ruin, and just science enough to show him how very little his science avails to save him from these "jagged wheels," or how very little his feeble reforms—opening the way often to a more dire disorder—or his transient "victories over nature," as he calls them, can avert the greatest, and sometimes the least, of her catastrophes. The thought of the immortality of the race, even if there were any hope or consolation in that, is as groundless as any other part of this sad speculation. What do "the merciless wheels" or "ponderous hammers" care for races? Of how many, in the past, has the die been broken and cast away! The race, as well as the individual, may be caught on some of these "jagged points," or crushed by the defacing "stamps" of these remorseless evolutions. We fly for refuge to the merciful anthropopathisms of the Bible: "He knoweth our frame; He remembers that we are dust; He careth for us." But what does nature know or care? It is all darkness—all horror. No retributions of religion are so terrible as this atheistic creed; no superstition presents so fearful a ground of alarm; for with these is ever associated some consoling idea of propitiation. A stern Judge, an unyielding moral law, a fearful danger as arising out of a relation having so much of moral dignity—these have in them, for a rational being, more of hope, less of pain and despair, than the crushing thought of having been brought into being, and made to suffer, for no end at all. Whoever sets out on the road that must ultimately lead to this, let him count the cost. Let him consult his guide-book, whatever it may be, to understand what he must come to when he makes his departure from the more serious forms of religious belief for the sake of easier creeds. What has been said will not be in vain, if such an impression shall have been left on any mind.

LECTURE II.

THE DENIAL OF THE SUPERNATURAL.

LECTURE II.

THE DENIAL OF THE SUPERNATURAL.

Aversion to the idea—Anthropopathism of the common infidel argument against a particular Providence—The alleged impossibility of the supernatural—The Divine constancy in nature—Moral power of a miracle—Men not afraid of nature—The soothing idea of physical law—Nature a screen between fallen man and Deity—Still, a fascination in the idea of the supernatural—Two kinds of incredibility: that of the sense, and that of the reason—Illustrations—The scene of the crucifixion—Moral reasons as affecting credibility—Moral power of the Biblical supernatural—Illustrations from Old Testament; from the New—Song of the Angels at the Nativity—Comparison between the Bible supernatural and that of all other "sacred books" and mythologies—Continual presence in the Bible of the moral sublime—The total absence of the supernatural, in such a disordered world as ours, would be the greatest wonder—The soul's demand for some extraordinary Divine manifestations—Childish argument: Nature all, therefore nothing above or beside nature—An eternal evolution self-evolved—Absurdities involved in such a view—The highest in the lowest—More out of less—Impossibility of the supernatural the staple of the rationalistic exegesis—The subjective truthfulness of the Bible involves the objective reality.

A CHIEF characteristic of the most modern form of unbelief is its strong aversion to the idea of the supernatural. It has lately taken a step beyond all former ones, in denying even its possibility. This cannot be called a feature of atheism strictly, for there all distinction between the natural and the supernatural wholly disappears with the divine idea. It is only, therefore, as connected with some form of professed theism that it is entitled to our attention: A God, so styled, but who interferes not now with nature, never will interfere, never has interfered, except, perhaps, at some indefinitely remote beginning brought in merely as a logical makeweight to some system of causation rising in the least conceivable degree above chance. The argument here sometimes assumes a quasi-religious form. God is too great to interfere with an order He has once established. He is too wise to interrupt a work so skilfully planned in the beginning. A particular providence, or any care for the individual, except as provided for in the great whole of things, is inconsistent with His sovereign dignity. He rules the world by laws. They are His ministers; any interference with them would imply a defect of knowledge or power in their selection and appointment. Thus viewed, all alleged miraculous intervention is petty, however grand it may sometimes seem to our finite view. Thus it is the divine honor they would defend as against the belittling conceptions of the narrow religionist. Sometimes it "apes humility." Man, especially the individual man, is too insignificant. It is presumptious in him to think that he is an object of the Divine concern, or that the settled course of things can ever be, in the least, affected by his wants and his prayers; it is all a wretched anthropopathy. Now to this it might easily be replied that the anthropomorphic reasoning is all the other way. It is our philosophic pietist who is making God altogether such an one as himself, needing machinery for the accomplishment of his purposes, and incapable of caring for the small, because occupied with the great totalities. Man can think of but one thing at a time, and this measure he applies to God, not perceiving that to depart one step from it gives an infinite range that may embrace an infinite multiplicity of objects as well as the smallest number. He fails to see that infinity and almightiness do, of themselves, demand the power of entering into the finite, of knowing it in its minutest aspects, of surveying it constantly in its partialities as well as in its totalities; in a word, of exercising the finite act when it pleases God, and even of thinking the finite thought, or feeling the finite feeling, whenever he chooses thus to enter into the mundane or the human sphere. One who cannot do this, cannot do "all things," as Job confesses, and is, therefore, neither almighty nor infinite. The infinite Word becomes flesh and dwells among us; the eternal Logos is ever sounding on in nature as when first uttered; it speaks in its minutest finities as well as in its greatest wholes. This is the grand Scripture doctrine which science fails to reach; this is the sublime equilibrium in the

Divine character which the Scripture everywhere so boldly maintains, and from which philosophy is ever wavering. A science unphilosophical as it is irreligious, repudiates it. It cannot rise to the conception of worlds transcending the physical, of spheres of being higher than nature, for which nature is made, for which its order is sustained, and for which it may be interrupted, if such a deviation of causality be demanded by a higher order and a higher law.

It would not be difficult thus to reply to the argument against miracles, or against a particular providence, as maintained by this semblance of theism. But the position now taken presents a somewhat different aspect. It is nothing less than a bold denial of the very possibility of the supernatural. The older English school of unbelievers never exactly reached this point. Hume's denial of miracles had reference solely to their incredibility on the ground of any sense evidence, the difficulty of proving them by any human testimony whose falsity would not be more credible than the alleged miracle itself. In other words, it was improbable, most improbable; unreasonable, apparently, but not impossible. This latter position is now taken with a blind hardihood that does not pretend to reason. It very cheaply assumes it as too plain for argument. No man of *sense*—we might take their word if confined to its most literal meaning—no man of sense, they say, can believe in the supernatural. The manner of the assertion, moreover, betrays feeling, a hearty dislike of the idea rather than the calm, philosophic temperament, or supreme love of truth that is so boasted of. The mask is thrown off. There is, indeed, a dishonest clinging to some fancied remnant of the theistic conception, but for all moral and religious purposes, it is that sinking of God in nature which no evasions of naming can differentiate from the blank atheistic denial. The older view, we may say, conceded a divine power over nature, though ever holding its exercise to be undivine and unreasonable; the latter denies the very power itself, because God and nature are one. The supernatural, therefore, is not only unreasonable, but impossible.

Both have their origin in fear—in that aversion to the thought of a personal God so deeply seated in the fallen human soul. It is not a speculative repugnance. It cannot be shown that there is anything irrational in the conception of an inconceivably great personality regarded as having power, intelligence, and will. The ground of fear is in the moral element which it is so difficult to keep separate from such a conception. Especially does this moral dread arise when the thought is entertained of some separated, isolated act, as it were, in which this personal relation of God to finite beings brings with it a sense of nearness, and so presents itself to us that we cannot thrust the thought away. In other words, this moral element most closely, and most immediately, connects itself with the sight, the belief, or even the conception of any miraculous or nature-transcending power. In proof of this, the appeal may be safely made to the human consciousness; though even evangelical men, so styled, have sometimes taken a different view. The value of miracles, it is maintained, is simply in their attestation. They have their place as credentials given to the first deliverers of a divine mission; they have simply a convincing and a silencing, but not strictly a moral power. The truth once given, or seen in its own intrinsic evidence, the sign that simply called attention to it, is no longer needed. We believe without it, it has been said; we believe better without it, and, therefore, nothing is really lost by overlooking the marvelous, or the alleged supernatural in the Scriptures; the essence of the truth remains.

It is true that miracles, if frequent, might lose their moral power, just as nature has done.

Had man continued holy, she, too, would have been religious, testifying to the "eternal power and Godhead" more powerfully than any miraculous or extraordinary display. The divine constancy in nature would then have furnished the adorable element. The change in the moral condition has wholly changed this aspect. Nature has become our screen, our veil from the insufferable brightness, our hiding-place from the terror of that idea of personality from which we shrink, even as Adam hid himself from the Lord God in the trees of the garden. God must now come to him in the thunder voice of supernatural manifestation; but even the effect of this would be lost in its frequency. Men would watch for sequences, they would hunt up coincidences, they would give them the soothing name of law, and thus would they make a new screen between themselves and God. We can see a reason why miracles should be rare; why more frequent in one age than in another; why they have characterized certain periods, especially those that belong to the earliest training of the human race; why at times they seem wholly withdrawn, and again appear with startling manifestations. The miracle may, indeed, be regarded chiefly in the light of an attestation demanded by some new message from above the sphere of the natural, or to arouse an age sinking into the grossest materialism. But still, along with its attesting it has ever its intrinsic moral power. Let there once be witnessed something which we are compelled to ascribe to a supernatural causation, and a new feeling, a religious feeling, is at once aroused, even though the attesting phenomena should be of the slightest kind. A personal will is showing itself; God is near; even the most devout soul has a new and startling sense of some divine presence. It is not the fear of the supernatural in itself. The same or a similar feeling may be awakened sometimes by witnessing remarkable phenomena, less usual, or more astounding, in nature itself, and when we think we know the causal sequences. In general, we are not afraid of nature; we are not afraid of law, that idol of our own creation which we are so fond of separating from the idea of a personal lawgiver. We can somehow take care of ourselves as against these; we feel more safe with them than with the thought of a personal providence; they do not so alarm us as the idea of falling into "the hands of the Living God." Even when there comes that awful cry of "the pestilence that walketh in darkness," we find an opiate in the idea of nature; we are relieved when our men of science talk to us so wisely of physical law. "Take heart," it is only something in the air or the water. That comforts, though we know nothing more. Especially is it so if the invading malady be more slow in its course, and its steps more visible, though actually more destructive than others that frighten us less. This is the secret of that panic that accompanies the dreaded name of cholera. It is something in the air, or in the water, to be sure. That gives some relief; but then it comes so suddenly, it strikes so irregularly, its movements are so inexplicable, its probabilities so baffle our most studied calculus; in a word, *we are so helpless*, we can do so little for ourselves, or for each other. If there is law in it, it is very much the same as though it were not. Something irresistible at least, something mysterious and unknown, is very near us. Hence at such times all men are religious, whether they choose to avow it or not. The speaker calls to mind a scientific man of some note who lately figured at a Tyndal dinner, and how frightened he was in the cholera season of 1849. How far it was a religious fear may not be confidently said; but certainly his science, much as it has been lauded, gave very little assurance to himself or others. He was a physician, too, confessing and bewailing the utter inadequacy of his skill to furnish any help. He gave up the patient. He should not, perhaps, be blamed for that; but then it should have taught him afterwards to be a little more merciful to his weaker fellow-creatures who lacked his scientific bravery, and who thought that there might possibly be some help in prayer. In these great and terrific manifestations, even of what we believe to be strictly physical forces, the awe of the supernatural is upon us. No amount of science gives assurance when the thunder crash is near, and the lightning bolt is falling at our feet, or its lurid flame is rising from our stricken place of shelter. It is the sense of helplessness which alarms, whilst it renders the ordinary distinction between the natural and the supernatural so powerless in soothing our fears. Calm reasoning, could we be calm, would tell us that the *probabilities* of harm are, in the long run, far greater from other physical causes that excite less emotion; but all that fails to give quiet. In a word, God is felt to be close at hand; our thought of the irresistible immediately takes the personal form, and no amount of science can drive it away. Now, in a still higher measure would this be felt at the sight of some appearance which we feel ourselves compelled to ascribe to a power above nature, or to a personal will near by, and intending the very thing our eyes behold. This moral power of a miracle as bringing nigh the thought of a personal God, is strikingly exemplified in the language of Peter at the sight of the miraculous draught of fishes, when he fell upon his knees and besought the Holy One to depart from him: ἔξελθε ἀπ' ἐμοῦ, "Go away from me for I am a sinner man, O Lord." Still more strange is it that it should be so, when the supernatural intervention is one of beneficence and salvation. Even that does not divest it of its moral awe; as when the waves were dashing over the ship, and the sleeping Christ awoke to still the storm. "They were astonished," say Matthew and Luke; "they were greatly afraid," says the more graphic Mark, and, on this occasion, with the deeper insight,—" They feared a great fear," and "They said one to another" "Who *then* is this." τίς ἄρα, as though the familiar Saviour had suddenly become strange and unknown; or as Matthew gives it, ποταπός ἐστιν οὗτος, "What kind of a being is this," whom "the winds and sea obey!"

In a world of holy unfallen beings, as has been already said, it would be the sight of nature's constancy which would chiefly inspire the religious feeling, but without that of personal dread. There would be no lessening of awe and sublimity in the contemplation of the physical movements, no burying of the divine idea, the ever-speaking word, the ever-living personal thought, in the dead notions of law and necessary sequence. Ever new, ever wonderful, ever harmonious would be the cosmical anthem—all *miranda*, if not *miracula* in the special sense we now attach to the controverted term. It would be a departure from such order, real or seeming, that would then suggest the godless thought, or carry with it the strange atheistical idea. Instead of the intervening " finger of God," as it appeared to the terrified Egyptian magicians, it would seem rather like a sign of returning chaos, as though the hand had let go the helm of the universe, or the Shekinah light were going out in the " Cosmical sanctuary," leaving it to darkness, confusion, and dismay. With man, in his God-forgetting state, the moral influence of a miracle, or of a seeming disturbance in nature, is just the reverse. When science is baffled, and law has ceased to soothe, and sequences seem broken, then it is that we are ready to cry out, " the finger of God," and to say with the ingenuous Peter: " Go away from us, O Lord, for we are sinful men."

And yet with all the moral dread, there is to the human mind a strange fascination in this idea of the supernatural. We cannot let it go.

Startling as is the thought of a personal God,

when it comes nigh to us, there are times when it is more tolerable to the thoughtful mind, even when not religious, than the iron-bound fixedness of an eternal, never-interrupted, never-to-be interrupted chain of physical sequences: A nature without beginning as it is without end, a fearful "perpetual motion," a horrible machine, such as Strauss describes, an everlasting syntagma, mindless, idealess, caring nothing for us, ever grinding on with its merciless laws—cause and effect—cause and effect, for ever evermore—suggesting nothing else than an eternal flow of sequences, in which we ourselves are indissolubly bound, with no hope of any existence ever rising above nature, or ever capable of drifting out of its right onward currents, or its circling vortexes. The thought is suffocating. Whatever may be the dread of religion in some of its aspects, we may well fly to it as a refuge from this stifling horror. Even superstition may be rationally welcomed as some relief from such a nightmare of the soul. It is in such an appeal to the deeper human consciousness we find a reply to both classes referred to—those who would represent a belief in the supernatural as simply alien and incredible, and those who go a step beyond, maintaining that the very idea involves an impossibility.

In regard to the first, a distinction should be made between two kinds of incredibility—that of the *sense*, and that of the *reason*. The first resolves itself into mere strangeness of event. There is no *reason* why it might not be, except that we have never seen it, and that stands to us in place of a reason. It need not be said how many events and phenomena, indubitable parts of nature as now known, would have to be rejected, if this mode of reasoning were strictly carried out by those who had never seen such phenomena, or to whose observations of nature they seemed to be in opposition. This has been much insisted upon by the opposers of Hume and the infidels of the eighteenth century. It is simply presented here as an illustration of that lower form of incredibility which I have styled the incredibility of the sense. Due weight is indeed to be given to it in argument. It justly demands unusual evidence for unusual events, whether alleged to be natural or supernatural—in some cases the very naturalness itself being *prima facie* more wonderful, that is, more incredible, than a supernatural causation. A strong reason, moral, spiritual, metaphysical, æsthetical even, may make the quiescence of nature, in a given case, more strange, that is, more increaible than its disturbance. The positive school, as it is called, makes sense the only arbiter, and with them perhaps, there is, in this matter, no further reasoning. They have settled it that there are no supersensual ideas, no intuitions, no aspirations—in a word, no supersensual world of being controlling all below, and for which all below has its existence. All such ideas are themselves supernatural, and therefore, in their view, incredible. For those, however, who believe in them, these higher faculties of the soul must be regarded as having also their claim to be heard. Viewed as separate from sense, or considered on a scale of higher probabilities, they, too, have an intrinsic reasonableness, demanding, in a given case, the strongest evidence on the other side, or against the happening of what they may seem to require, even though involving a disturbance of the usual sequence of events.

And this is what we mean by the credibility or incredibility of the reason. It is that view, or those considerations which, aside from any strangeness of the sense, would warrant us in pronouncing an alleged event, whether of an ordinary or extraordinary kind, rational and therefore credible. It is not an assuming of its reality, but only of such a connection with a higher state of things perfectly rational and conceivable, as might change the scale and preponderance of evidence as addressed to the sense-transcending faculties. Take the vivid gospel narrative of the crucifixion. Keep the mind fixed upon the central fact as presenting the, essential idea. A holy man—the holiest man ever known on this sin-polluted earth—suspended on the cross. By wicked hands is He taken, crucified, and slain. He is enduring inconceivable agony. His malignant murderers are feasting their eyes upon the spectacle. They taunt Him with His helplessness, saying : "Come down now from the cross, if Thou be indeed the Christ, the Son of God." It is a challenge to the Eternal Father. It is a charging Him with indifference towards the holy sufferer. In bitter mockery they give him vinegar to drink, mingled with gall. His dying thirst unquenched, He utters a mighty wailing cry of desolation, and gives up the ghost. Now connect this awful scene with the perfectly rational conception of a Holy One in the heavens—One who loves righteousness and hates wrong with a divine intensity—One who possesses almighty power and infinite goodness. He is beholding this demonic spectacle; it lies right beneath His holy eye. Nature is under His control, as it is, though in a far less degree, under the supernatural control of man. Now we cannot say that He will certainly interfere with it; we may not deny His existence, or doubt His power, or charge Him with indifference, if He does not supernaturally interfere with it. He may even have great moral or nature-transcending purposes that may prevent His interfering with it, or making any special manifestation respecting it. Good men have been put to death most unjustly; they have died in agonies of flame and crucifixion; they have suffered, and nature has been silent; no sign has come from the superhuman or supernatural sphere. So there may be reasons why God should not interfere with it in this case, or even give any sign of His beholding or His displeasure. It is, therefore, not incredible that the sun should shine calmly in the heavens, or go placidly down in presence of such a scene, or that nature should give no visible intimation of its sympathy, or of any sympathy on the part of Him who sits above. We may say, too, that should such sign be given, it would be strange to the sense, and, so far, have about it a sense-incredibility. But is there not a strangeness, an incredibility, in the other aspect, that may overpower this sense-incredibility, or become so strong, in a given case, as to make it more easy to believe that the rocks should be rent, that the earth should tremble, or that the sun should be darkened, than that nature and the infinitely Holy One who sits above in the high and holy place, should manifest no sympathy, no sign even of His witnessing presence. It must be a *moral* reason in either case, whether for the wondrous appearing, or for what may be the still more wondrous withholding. The appeal is made to a higher faculty than the sense. There may be answers to it; but surely these higher powers, the reason, the conscience—in a word, the consideration of a sphere of being above the physical, should have their weight in judging of the question, and the whole measure of credibility. It is the exceeding greatness of the moral reason connected with the alleged event which may be regarded as affecting the scale, so as to make it easy of belief to the mind deeply impressed with it. In other words, for souls accessible to this higher evidence, the moral strangeness in the one aspect might more than balance the physical strangeness so much insisted on in the other and narrower view.

A moral reason, or an impressive moral fact, joined with an alleged miraculous or supernatural event; every thinking mind must see that this being the case or not, must have an important bearing on the question of credibility. It is here we find the striking difference between the Bible marvelous and the Bible supernatural, and that of all other religions and mythologies with which some are so fond of comparing it. There is a moral sublimity about it found nowhere else, and which gross ignorance alone, or still more gross unfairness, can refuse to acknowledge. Compare the Bible myths, if any insist upon so calling them, with Greek myths, or Hindoo myths, or Scandinavian myths, or any wonders fancied or deciphered from Egyptian or Assyrian monuments. The literary men among us who have so much to say about the Vedas, and the Shastras, and the primitive fire-worship, and the "tracing to these sources of all Christian theology," and of all scriptural mythology—let them bring on their authorities. If their ignorance of the Vedas, and of the Eastern Scriptures, is not greater than their ignorance of the Bible, let them cite book, chapter, section, verse, and lay them side by side with the Old and New Testaments. Or let them bring the best things their knowledge, their taste, their criticism, or their philosophy can select from these vaunted sources, and then let the Christian—even the unlearned Christian—confront them, singly or collectively, with spiritual gems, and spiritual wonders, gathered from our holy book. Nothing could be more decisive; nothing would so effectually put an end to this shallow literary babble now breeding so much ignorant scepticism; nothing would so thoroughly dissipate the foolish prating about Christ and Confucius, Christ and Buddha, which is now kept up by our wise lecturers, and on the slightest connections, whether it be the discovery of a Babylonian tablet with its monstrous imagery, and still more monstrous record, if rightly deciphered, or the finding of a fire-hook dug up from the site of ancient Troy. Especially may such a challenge be made in respect to the Bible supernatural as compared with that which is found in the mythological writings, hymns, or traditions of all other nations. If anything can be called universal, innate, common to all religious and even to all serious human thought, it is this tendency to the reception of the supernatural. The inference from it is a most important one, and we commend it to those who have so much to say about the natural and the universal religion. But it is this striking difference between the Bible supernatural and all other wonders to which special attention is here asked. Note the monstrosity, the grotesqueness, the sheer fancifulness, the absence of satisfying moral reasons, that everywhere characterize the heathen mythologies. It is not only that moral reasons are absent, but that there is in them, for the most part, *no reason at all.* It is this more than anything else that constitutes their incredibility. How different the Bible marvelous! The moral is everywhere, not only present, but predominant. This so takes possession of the mind that the physical strangeness falls in the background, if it does not wholly disappear. Hence it is that the Bible supernatural comes to seem natural, if we may express it thus paradoxically. It is a *nodus vindice dignus.* It seems just the right thing, the fit and proper thing, the thing to be expected, the thing whose absence, it might almost be said, would seem strange in the midst of such sublime moral accompaniments. It is an ignorant slander, as uttered by some of our literary men, that the Christian reads his Bible with the same *unreasoning* confidence in its wonders as the Hindoo feels in the perusal of his sacred books, or in reciting his traditional legends. They know nothing about the Bible who say this, as indeed they know very little about the writings with which they so flippantly compare it. Crude monstrosities, unmeaning transformations, grotesque developments, hideous physical generations, which some take great pains to call incarnations in order to cast dishonor upon the Scripture doctrine of the Logos—grossly animal metamorphoses, all taking place without any moral reason, without any reason at all, without even any known physical analogy, are thus unblushingly compared with the Christian and Biblical marvelous, in which the very impression of the miraculous disappears before the moral and spiritual awe. This explains why these Bible wonders, when read by the most intellectual and cultured minds—equal in this respect to the highest of those who make the charge—carry with them such a marvelous air of truthfulness, such a serene and majestic impression of reality. It is this state of soul, and the discernment of this peculiar character in the Holy Scripture, that makes the wide difference between men like Augustine, Anselm, Hooker, Bacon, Cudworth, Edwards, Hall, Coleridge, Foster, Neander, Maurice, Newman, Isaac Taylor, Montalambert, Guizot, on the one side, and the admired writers in some of our monthlies on the other. Certainly the men I have mentioned, with all the hindrances of their age that may be conceded in respect to some of them, were as well qualified to discern the monstrous, the legendary, the absurd, as Mr. Emerson, or Mr. Oliver Wendell Homes, or Mr. Bayard Taylor, with all the reputation for genius and talent which is conceded to them.

As an evidence of this divine impress upon the supernatural of the Scriptures, take the account of Moses' vision of the burning bush, as given in Exodus iii. How destitute of all the higher moral emotional must be the soul that can read it without a feeling of its calm, unutterable sublimity! How does every Greek legend pale before it in this aspect of scenic power, even if we take nothing else into the account. Brief as it is, what other myth, so called, can compare with it in its awful, graphic vividness. And yet what an absence of the mere *wonder-making*, or the sensational in style! But this is only the outward accompaniment. It is the moral idea, the moral reason—that which other legends so much lack, unless as invented for them by unnatural or far-fetched accommodation—which gives it its ineffable sanctity and power. The very simplicity of the narration is the strongest evidence of its truthfulness; the sensational is hushed, the awe upon the soul is too great for any mere emotional utterance. "And Moses said, I will now turn aside and see this great sight:" the flaming bush alone in the weird desert—steadily "burning, but not consumed." There is the moral here, the moral sublime transcending the physical sublime, the moral awe transcending the physical wonder, and making it seem like nature itself attesting the presence of its Lord. It has this moral power as the symbol of "the ever-living God," as connected with the great name of Jehovah which some have sought so ineffectually, yet with such strange zeal, to bring out of the Egyptian darkness, or to deduce its high spiritual significance from the most unspiritual of all the ancient mythologies. It is the proclamation of the eternal self-existence, the I AM, the timeless being, ὁ ὤν, καὶ ὁ ἦν, καὶ ὁ ἐρχόμενος, who *is*, and *was*, and *is to come*. "Burning ever, but not consumed;" what a power in this language of symbol, as proved by the inadequacy of other language, written or articulate, to express by any one of its imperfect tense forms, or by all of them conjoined, this timeless idea! Another example of this peculiarity is presented to us in the thunders of Sinai, the flaming mount, the appalling darkness into which Moses ascends, the awful voice, at which "the people trembled," and "removed afar off," and "entreated that the word should not be spoken to them any more." How life-like, and yet how ineffably sublime! How much there was here of the strictly natural, the volcanic, or the electric, we may not know, nor does it much concern us to inquire. The Scripture makes little of the distinction on which the modern mind so much insists. It blends the great and the terrible of both departments in its representations of the power and presence of

God. But here comes in again the moral greatness of the scene. It is something beyond, either the natural, or the supernatural regarded merely in its effect upon the physical world. It is the spiritual sublimity we recognize in the *reason* of the event as transcending both. It is the occasion of giving a law to a people chosen from among the nations then fast sinking into polytheism and idolatry—chosen and preserved as a *world-people*, the world prophets, the keepers of truth, and of the glorious Messianic promise in which " all the families of the earth should be blessed "—in which *we* are blessed—from whom has come an influence beyond all the power of Greek and Roman literature, and by which our modern world has been so greatly elevated and transformed. It is this which makes it seem easy to us—rational, credible, most appropriate, most harmonious, when we read the moral message of which this superhuman scenery was the accompaniment : " And God spake all these words saying, I am Jehovah thy God. Thou shalt have no other gods before me. Thou shalt not make to thee any image or any likeness of anything that is in heaven above, or that is in the earth beneath, or that is in the waters below the earth. Thou shalt not bow down thyself to them ; for I, Jehovah thy God, am a jealous God

—a holy God—visiting iniquity unto the third and fourth generations of them that hate me, and showing mercy unto thousands of them that love me and keep my Commandments." It is to this moral sublime that Moses appeals, Deut. iv.: "For what nation is so great, that hath God so nigh unto them; and what nation is so distinguished that hath statutes and judgments so righteous. Keep in mind the day that thou stoodest before the Lord thy God in Horeb, and ye came near and stood under the mountain, and the mountain burned with fire unto the very heart of the heavens, with clouds, also, and thick darkness, and the Lord spake unto you out of the fire; ye heard a voice, but saw no similitude. Take ye, therefore, good heed unto yourselves, lest ye corrupt yourselves, and make you the likeness of any figure, male or female, or lest ye lift up your eyes unto heaven, and behold the moon and the stars, even all the host of heaven, and be led to worship them—take good heed to yourselves, for ye saw no manner of similitude on the day when the Lord spake unto you in Horeb, out of the midst of the fire." Where did the legendary ever so combine the supernatural and the moral, the awful and the familiar? When did a Greek myth-maker, or myth-collector, when did a Greek lawgiver make such an appeal to a people, citing the most wonderful event in their history as a well known statistical fact entering so deeply into their moral and religious consciousness? And where, too, it may well be asked, could be found the moral ground of such a consciousness in any of their cotemporary surroundings, if it had not come from some such stupendous revelation?

The Mosaic conception of Deity, the idea of the timeless I AM, of the God who has no similitude in heaven or earth, this from the Egyptians! A thought so ineffably pure and holy plagiarized from a people whose imagery buries out of sight every moral or spiritual conception the most Bible-hating imagination could possibly trace in their sensual nature-worship, and their degraded animal forms. Let the rationalist, so called, believe this, if he can.

Or come we down to the New Testament marvelous; take the narrative the most astounding, the most legendary in its outer aspect of them all—the guiding star of the Wise Men, as Dr. Upham has so powerfully presented it in his wonderful book—along with it the Song of the Angels, the light that shone so suddenly around the adoring shepherds, the choral anthem that seemed to come from "the heavenly places:" *Gloria in excelsis*—" Glory to

God in the highest; on earth peace, good-will to men." As the marvelous merely, as the rapt ideal, how transcendingly sublime! Where do we find anything like it in other legendary lore? How would it strike us, even in this aspect, if it had come upon us in the reading of any Greek or Hindoo myth, in some legend of Jupiter, Hercules, Brahma, Vishnu, Thor, or Woden? But now look at it in connection with that still more glorious moral conception which it attests. View it as bearing witness to the incarnation of the Logos, that most wondrous fact in the evolutions of the world—that most wondrous event, as then manifested in the developments of human history. It is the birth of the Redeemer, the hero of the Protevangel, the mighty champion against the powers of evil, the glorious Messiah, then humanly born in Bethlehem, "least of the cities of Judah," (as earth is least, it may be, among the planetary worlds,) but of whose spiritual and moral kingdom there was to be no end. Is it incredible, viewed in itself, that to such a fact, such an ideal even, there should be an attestation drawn from a higher sphere—if it is not irrational to believe in such higher sphere—and giving a reason and a meaning to the physical wonder itself? Gloria in excelsis. " Glory to God in the highest; on earth peace, good-will to men." This unreal! what, then, is real? This to be thrown away as belonging to the world of dreams, and the puzzling material shadows that come and go, appear and disappear, upon this low stage of being—Strauss, Renan, Hume, Voltaire, Tyndall, Darwin, Huxley, apes, gorillas—all these having a veritable place *in rerum natura!* "Glory to God in the highest; on earth peace, good-will to men;" such a song from the supernal sphere falling upon the human sense; it cannot be, says the sceptic, it cannot be, for it was never heard before, it has not been heard since, and therefore no evidence can prove it. But imagine now—and it is a perfectly rational exercise of this high faculty—imagine now a being who had never seen a world like this, so full of evil, physical evil, physical irregularity as it appears —so abounding in moral obliquity, in madness, crime, in all unreason, in all spritual deformity— could either sense or reason credit it?

The peculiarity to which attention is called appears throughout the Bible. In all its supernatural, this moral ground and moral reason may be distinctly seen. There is nothing in it capricious, reasonless, monstrous, or grotesque. Now, whatever may be the condition of other worlds, the one in which we live is certainly full of moral disorder, and there would seem to be a propriety that the physical, in such a world, should present some reflection of the spiritual confusion. Given, then, the idea of a personal God, of a holy God, loving righteousness, and hating sin—a deity in whose eyes the physical is subordinate to the moral, and has its value only as a disciplinary and probationary aid to a higher spiritual excellence; given this, which no one can call irrational, and we may boldly reverse the position which some so confidently assume. It would be the rarity of the supernatural that would be the real wonder. The utter silence of nature; that would be the real miracle. Even in such a morally disordered world, regularity in physical phenomena would still have a ground in the reason; it would be demanded for the ordinary government of rational action; but the total absence of any sign from the higher sphere attesting the presence of the denied or the contemned lawgiver, that would be a thing most wonderful, most incredible. And to this corresponds the natural feeling of the human soul. Why has a belief in the supernatural, I ask again, been so universal? To fallen beings there is, indeed, a dread in the thought of a personal intervening deity, but this is overpowered, at times, by the still more alarming thought of there being nothing above us that concerns itself with the affairs of men. When crime unpunished fills the land, when cruelty, injustice, oppression, are everywhere triumphant; when the predominance of wealth and capital are crushing labor to the earth; when the poor cry out, and our boasted science of political economy, with all its vaunted remedial powers, is found an utter failure; when ambition, with its mighty standing armies, is filling the earth with groans and blood, and all the visible laws of nature seem pressed into the service of those who perpetrate such enormities; when "men are made as the fishes of the sea, taken with the angle, caught in the net, gathered in the drag;" when all mere humanitarian reforms have proved their falsity, or have exceeded in mischief the very evils they were proposed to remedy; when the last great boast of democracy is showing itself a failure, as well as the monarchies and aristocracies and priesthoods that preceded it; when "earth seems given into the hands of the wicked"—how instinctively does the mind rise to something higher than nature! "O that Thou wouldst rend the heavens and come down;" the cry is in the soul, if not uttered by the voice, or its meaning distinctly conceived by the understanding. Though we may not reason clearly about it, it is felt that it is the highest reason that prompts it. The politician, the editor, even the infidel statesman, seem sometimes strangely driven to the utterance of language that can have no other meaning. It is all inconsistent, indeed, hypocritical perhaps, in some of its aspects, but still in deference to this irrepressible feeling. There *must* be an interposition, somehow and somewhere, in favor of right. If questioned as to their distinct meaning in such utterances, they would doubtless have over again the old babble of intervention by social laws, or natural laws, as though nature herself were gentle, long-suffering, merciful, righteous, opposed to wrong; but it is an intervention after all, something that would not happen in the course of things as they were going on, and the idea cannot stop short of the supernatural. The expectation is utterly reasonless, or it must be supposed that somewhere the switch is turned by an unseen hand; at some link or nexus in the lower sphere of nature and humanity comes in the interference that receives its command from the higher order and the higher law. "I tremble for my country," says Jefferson, "when I remember that God is just and that His vengeance will not sleep for ever." However little he may have individually meant by this, it came from him impulsively as the prophet of the human soul. Sometimes the reverse thought sorely tries the believer's faith: "Art Thou not from everlasting Jehovah, my God, my Holy One? Thou art of purer eyes than to behold evil; wherefore lookest Thou, then, upon them who deal treacherously, and holdest Thy peace when the wicked devoureth the man that is more righteous than he?" Even to the Christian it is the rarity of the supernatural that seems the real paradox: "Why standest Thou afar off?" Why does not God oftener speak to us? Why are the heavens so still? Instead of there being apparently so little of intervention in the affairs of men, why is there not a great deal more than has ever been recorded either in Scripture or in mythology? The pious soul reconciles itself to it, but it is only on the ground of faith, rising above both sense and reason: "Clouds and darkness are round about Him, but judgment and truth are the foundation of His throne."

But the most modern infidelity, as I have said, takes a step beyond this. The supernatural, it affirms, is not simply *incredible*, difficult of belief, requiring strong and rare evidence, but absolutely *impossible*. It would not be easy to say on what rational grounds this dictum rests. As commonly used, it is a sheer assumption. It has no reason in it. It is equivalent to denying that there is anything above nature, older than nature, or from which it comes. It has no reason, we say, for it is the annihilation of reason regarded as anything else than itself a product of nature, as thought and consciousness are affirmed to be. Now reason, if there be any such thing, must be supreme. It must be primeval, first of all. "The Logos" must be "in the beginning" or it has no true existence. That to which we give the name of reason is, on the other hypothesis, but a shadow, a transient reflection from the physical, and can, therefore, never rise above it, or pronounce any judgment about it as rational or irrational. Whenever, therefore, any formal argument is attempted here, the assumption becomes immediately manifest in all its baldness. It comes to this: Nature is all; therefore there can be nothing else. Most lucid enthymeme! But that is all they can make of it. They avoid any objection drawn from the human faculties, by simply turning man himself into nature. By this arbitrary and impudent assumption, the human thought, consciousness, reason, immediately become products of nature, and even some divines, through a prejudice in favor of their own narrow definition of the supernatural, are forced to the same conclusion. Our souls are in the machinery as much as our bones. The passengers in the railroad train, with all their ideals, all their speculations, all their politics, morals, religions even, are as purely physical forces, physical movements, as the grass growing in the fields by which they are so rapidly passing. The engineer is himself but a part of the machinery. Nay more, the very inventor of the engine, and even the invention itself, is as much an inseparable part of nature as the boiling water or the hissing steam. When we depart, however, in the least from this sheer petitio principii *that nature is all*, we are at once in a region that carries our reasoning fearfully far and fearfully high. If nature is not all, then it may be a small portion of the whole, and not only a small, but a very inferior thing, whose fixedness or mutability can have their value only in relation to some sphere or world above. In this crude assumption nature is not defined. If it is meant as only another name for being in general, or for the whole system of things including a supreme mind and a will as well as a supreme force, then it becomes a childish logomachy. It is the shallowest truism when we say that the laws of the cosmos, thus regarded, cannot be broken. It becomes simply a name for God's government, and all rational minds must assent to the proposition that in it there can be nothing capricious, nothing without reason. "All things were made by the Logos, and without him was there nothing made that was made." If there is any seeming deviation, any interruption of the course of the visible nature, it is in obedience to some higher law of the supernatural world. We may even suppose that such deviation from the ordinary visible is brought about by a transcending personality, acting directly upon, and through, deeply interior laws, or forces in nature herself—such springs or cogs as only operate, or approach, or come in contact, when the hour is struck, though lying long quiescent in the ordinary movement of the clock, or silently nearing each other in that far down region to which no science can penetrate. The secret of such forces may be known to higher intelligences, whether God, or angels, or human beings supernaturally endowed with a deeper insight, and employing it, as ordinary men do in their ordinary interferences with the more superficial movements of nature,—turning it *from* what it would have done, or *to* what it would not have done, had it been left to itself. Some religious minds might, perhaps, be afraid of this, as confusing the distinction between the natural and the supernatural. But we need not concern ourselves about words here. It would still be miraculous, wonderful, full of awe. It would be all the same, so far as that moral power is concerned on which we have been insisting. It would be accompanied by the same fear of something personal above or beyond nature. It might even be thought to carry with it a greater alarm, making nature itself a more fearful thing, as having, in its deep interior, hidden causalties unknown to our keenest science, yet furnishing a means of startling efficiencies to beings of a higher knowledge, or to forces connected with a higher human psychology.

But there are other irrationalities resulting from the assumption that nature is all. The statement of them may not seem obvious, since the position assailed is of a kind so strange, so absurdly facile, that it would seem incapable of refutation as it is of defence. Let us take the infidel scientist's own view of it as an uninterrupted, or never interfered with, evolution, or *coming out* of things—ever coming out from that which is lowest in the remotest past, and to whose primeval emptiness nothing has ever really been added. Then, if nature is all, it is an eternal evolution, an eternal *coming out*, having no other end than such evolving. It is an eternal coming out that never, in fact, does come out, or that goes back as fast as it does come out. There is nothing *finished* in it, and there is excluded the thought of any *perfect*, or τελειον, anything finished in any world above to which this eternal evolution is subservient. There are no such world, or worlds, above it, for which nature was made, or for the sake of which it is thus evolving, unwinding, until it is all spent, or, like some coiled spiral, winding back again to the starting-point, if starting-point is conceivable, and so on, and so on, evolutions of evolutions, for ever and for evermore. There are, strictly, no ends in the universe transcending the working of this purely physical machinery thus ever evolving *for the sake of evolving.** There are, then, no other ends,

---

* A higher world than the physical necessary to explain the physical: This is the idea on which we so much insist, and it is gratifying to find it clearly and conclusively stated by so good an authority as the editor of "The Nation," No. 517 (May 17, 1875), page 367, where he says: "The affirmation that this physical world has also a moral meaning (that is, finds its end in a moral world above it), is one that no argument drawn from purely physical science can impugn." It is, however, but another mode of expressing a thought drawn from very ancient writings. Physical science, "the science of *change* and *motion*," as Aristotle defined it, cannot determine its own place; it cannot say what may or what may not be above it in the immovable spheres. Therefore it is that this great thinker assigns to it a rank below the *mathematical* and the *theological*: τί βέλτιστον ; φυσική, μαθηματική, θεολογική ; See the question briefly stated, *Arist. Metaph.* Lib. x. (xi.), ch. 7.

such as ends moral, artistic, ideal, ineffable. There are, in truth, no ends at all. There can be none; for that which ever terminates in the process of its own evolution is no end; and if there is no end, then no idea; if no idea, then no law. Not only is there no Logos in the beginning, there is none that can ever be evolved.

The incredibility of the supernatural, or, in other words, the just demand of strong evidence in particular cases, presents a fair ground of argument. That evidence, however, has been supplied. In regard to its weight there is matter of controversy, but here believers have triumphantly met the infidel arguments in the old debates, and are prepared to meet them again. The field of conflict has in no respect changed. Such a fact as the Resurrection of Christ was not, indeed, to be lightly received; but the proof demanded has been furnished, not only from the overwhelming cotemporaneous testimony of the most unimpeachable witnesses, sealed by lives of heroic endurance, and by deaths of cruel martyrdom, but from the standing spiritual miracle which it has wrought in the world—the supernatural, unearthly light that came forth from that sepulchre, and of which our own eyes and our own hearts are still witnesses. That controversy, we say, stands as it did before;

but here comes up a new form of denial, all the more stubborn and audacious in proportion to its utter want of rational ground. The Resurrection of our Saviour never took place; no miraculous event, as recorded in the Bible, ever had any objective reality. And why? Not simply on the ground of strangeness, or any measurable *incredibility* of sense, but because a miracle, a wonder in nature, any deviation from her ordinary visible course, and that, too, as falling under the exceedingly limited observation of our positive philosopher, is absolutely *impossible*. This is the new position that now meets us everywhere. It is coolly assumed by the scientist without the shadow of an argument. With still less of reason, if possible, it is echoed by many in the literary world. But most irrational of all is the use made of it by a certain class of Biblical critics. This sheer assumption they take as the ground of all their interpretations. For them it is enough to disprove the verity, or the authenticity, even, of any portion of the Bible, that there is in it any mention of a supernatural event, whatever the moral ground, or the accompanying moral reasons. Anything prophetic is at once set down as evidence of a later date, and rejected as a matter of course. Here they take their stand with a stubbornness all the greater as it is opposed to the critical as well as to the moral reason. The supernatural is impossible, and, therefore, there need be no further argument about the passage. This is not the place for dwelling critically on such a position. It may only be said that it marks the inconsistency of a certain class of men who will not let the Scriptures alone, and yet deny the very characteristics that would chiefly seem to make them worthy of our study. It is a blind overlooking of the very elements in which they differ from all else called mythical or legendary. It is a denial of that patent moral character which is their standing peculiarity, and without which they sink below the rank of myths into sheer circumstantial and statistical lying, a deliberate imposture—a charge which, at this day, the wisest Rationalist shrinks from making against them. Such is the treatment they give to a book for which they profess a high respect, but which cannot be thus interpreted without violating their own famous canon in disregarding what is most characteristic of the Bible, and its high claim as a supernatural revelation. We cannot rightly interpret Homer without conceding to him a belief in his own mythology. But here is the difference between the Scriptures and all other narrations of the marvelous. Once concede a subjective truthfulness to the Biblical writers,

5

and the objective verity of details thus given becomes irresistible. The only alternative of escape from it is by taking the ground which very few are now willing to take, that the Scriptures are designedly and statistically false; in other words, the most circumstantial and studied imposition ever presented to the credulity of mankind.

The main object in this lecture has been the consideration of two main infidel assumptions, the *incredibility* and the *impossibility* of the supernatural. The latter, it cannot be too often repeated, is put forth without even the semblance of an argument, and yet with a confidence that could only be felt in a mathematical demonstration. Nature is all. There are no other spheres of being, no ends transcending its endless and aimless evolutions. Let the narrowness, as well as the audacity, of this assumption be duly considered, and the whole fabric of unbelief built upon it falls to the ground. It becomes a *tohu* and *bohu*, empty, foundationless, formless, and void. The idea of possible spheres of being higher than nature, and for which nature itself is made, at once sweeps it all away. In the clear light of such a thought is seen the utter perversity, as well as narrowness, of the lower or solely physical view. "O we of little faith! wherefore did we ever doubt?" Such is the feeling when the mist clears up, and we get into a way of thinking so much purer and easier than the one that tortures the intellect as well as the affections. Depart from this, and there is no stopping-place short of the horrors of Strauss, with his dream of the iron wheels, that, in respect to gloomy grandeur, might almost seem to vie with the visions of Ezekiel or of Dante. On the other hand, begin with this, and all is clear. Nature has a meaning and a value. It becomes itself a higher department of the universe just in proportion as it is raised to this higher office. It gets its true meaning when thus regarded as subservient to more glorious spheres of being partially revealed in the Scriptures, measurably thinkable by the human mind, and suggestive of still higher things that " eye hath not seen, nor ear heard, nor the heart of man conceived."

LECTURE III.

THE COSMICAL ARGUMENT—WORLDS IN SPACE.

LECTURE III.

THE COSMICAL ARGUMENT—WORLDS IN SPACE.

Cosmical Argument; Worlds in Space—Astronomical Objection—Its pressure—Trine aspect of the Universe—The believer charged with narrow conceptions — The three dimensions of being—The additions physical science has made to our knowledge, mainly mathematical—Question of planetary life still unsettled—Ancient ideas of cosmical immensity—Relative distances—Emotional feeling of greatness not affected by number—Idea of law in the Scriptures, and as held by the most contemplative ancient minds—The stars as mighty beings—Modern conception that of endless repetition: less favorable to the unity of the cosmos than the ancient, though the latter was grounded on a more limited fact knowledge—Idea of great world times—How affected by modern science—St. Augustine—Reconciliations between science and the Bible—Their small value—No science in the Bible, a proof of a higher inspiration—Scientific pretensions of other books called sacred—Grandeur of the Bible language—Heavens in the plural—Eternities in the plural—New knowledge as a ground of new interpretations—New Testament interpreting the Old—Mounting or germinant senses in distinction from double senses, or the cabalistical—Advance of physical knowledge may have a similar effect—New expansions of old ideas.

THE "astronomical objection" to Christianity, as it is most commonly called, is the one probably that presses hardest upon the thoughtful mind. It addresses itself so powerfully to the imagination, and through it, at times, bewilders and amazes, if it does not wholly silence, that stronger faculty, the reason. It comes to us under two aspects, to which we may give the names of the stellar and the cosmical. The one confounds us with the array of worlds supposed to be, like our earth, the abodes of life and ration-

(103)

ality, and, therefore, diminishing to a great, if not an infinite, degree, the importance which the Scriptures seem to attach to man. The other has more reference to the origin of the cosmos and its vast times, as supposed to be inconsistent with the scriptural account of creation. The first dates mainly from the discoveries of the telescope. The other goes much farther back. Cosmical speculations about the origin of the world, the eternity of the world, its material and dynamical causalities, many of them strikingly similar to some that are now most rife, belong to ancient times—to very ancient times. Thoughtful men have been always thinking about these things. Even "the infinity ot worlds" was a very old speculation. We might call them the space and time aspects, and it was first thought best to present them in two separate lectures, with separate titles. The ideas, however, so intermingled themselves, that one general title seemed most appropriate, though regarded as embracing two principal divisions. The name "cosmical," then, may be taken as the common title to both lectures, or one more applicable still may be found in an expression I have ventured to employ, though quite unusual. As extending beyond both space and time, and ascending to the still higher conception of rank or order of being, permit me to call it the three-fold, or TRINE ASPECT OF THE UNIVERSE,—a term to be more fully explained in its applications.

The believer in the Bible is charged with entertaining narrow views of the cosmos, or of the great whole of being. Science has introduced enlarged conceptions destructive of the old faith. It is no longer possible to believe as Bacon did. Even Newton can no more be cited, as formerly, in proof that one may hold to the Scriptures, and yet be a man of profound and elevated thought. But there are other aspects to such a charge, that might not only change, but invert its force. Of Newton it might be said that he, at least, lived at a time when astronomical science had furnished all the important materials for the boasting inference before alluded to. It may be safely affirmed, that, so far as concerns the question we are now contemplating, nothing that has since been discovered gives the most modern astronomer here any advantage over the devout Catholic Copernicus, or the pious Protestants, Kepler, Euler, and Newton. Two more distant planets have been barely seen; a swarm of worthless asteroids, and a few more of that still inexplicable class of bodies, the comets, have been added to the catalogues, but their bearing on the question is too small for computation. It could not have driven Newton from his faith in the Scriptures. The new light which burst upon the world through the telescope had been anticipated by Kepler. To the others, whose names have been mentioned, it was clearly suggestive of every enlarged conclusion that has been, or is now, drawn from that discovery.

Against such a charge we need not hesitate to use the shield of such authorities. But the question after all remains, On which side does the narrowness really exist? Far be it from me to rail at science or scientific men; but certainly there does sometimes reveal itself among the more boasting scientists an incapacity for moral and spiritual views that in their intrinsic grandeur, throw all physical discovery into the shade. In proof of such blindness, there might be cited this exceedingly narrow notion that nature is all, and that weak truism so confidently built upon it, that, therefore, there can be nothing which is not nature—that is, no supernatural. The charge against the religionist seems plausible. No other world in space than this little earth of ours! What a paltry conception! But take now another view. Look away from this thinnest aspect of mere width, this outstretching space view with its possible, and, as many analogies would tend to show, its probable sameness of conditions, as nascent, growing, decaying, progressive, retrograding,—all alike essentially, as all springing from one mother nebula, one common causal development, unvaried, as they would have us believe, by causes or fiats of a higher order. Look above this mere physical plane of *worlds beyond worlds*, to what we have called the rank-aspect of *worlds above worlds*. The question then would stand thus: No other world or plane of being than the physical, ever returning into itself, and having no ends out of itself, no aims above itself; no other world, or worlds, than those we can survey with our telescopes, or peer into with our microscopes—no higher moral or spiritual sphere for which the physical exists, and without which it has no other than a physical value, that is, relatively no value at all! What an exceeding narrowness is here? The first is simply a deficiency of fact knowledge, and may, therefore, be enlarged; the other blindness keeps the eye closed to all that light within which reveals to us the paltriness of the physical, even in its largest spatial and dynamical extent, when there is acknowledged nothing beyond and above it. It is thus that this doctrine, which makes nature all, so stultifies itself. Viewed from a higher point of contemplation, it shrinks to a narrowness, a thinness rather, beyond anything that may be charged upon a limited space conception of the sense universe. The vast surface width that it gives the cosmos is all the more unmeaning, all the more void of reason, from its want of depth and height.

As the idea of geometrical magnitude demands for its perfection the three dimensions of length, breadth, and altitude, so the true conception of the universe does not become full and satisfying, until it assumes in our minds a trine aspect. Up and down are, indeed, relative terms, and so Solomon must have regarded them when he speaks of "the heaven and the heaven of heavens." So all thinking men from Solomon to Aristotle and Newton, have ever regarded them. But the ideas they typify are real. It is felt that there must be, in the great system of things, a profundity corresponding to the altitude, an evil to the good, a darkness, too, a risk and a loss, forming a counterpart to the light, the hope, and the glory. The cosmical view must tend to this rounded completeness, unless some lower form of being obtains an interest, scientific or otherwise, that relatively obscures the higher. Thus it is very possible that the unscientific mind, or a thoughtful soul possessing a very limited sense knowledge, may have this trine conception more perfectly developed, that is, in better proportions, than another far excelling in the amount of physical science, if such science confine the thoughts to one usurp'ng nd absorbing view. These three aspects, then, may be tersely denoted as the *cosmos in space*, the cosmos in time, the cosmos, or the universe, in its unfolded and unfolding ranks of being, as ascending in their physical, moral, spiritual, hyperphysical scales of gradation; the first analogous to *width* or *breadth*, the second to *length*, the third to altitude, not in space-dimension, but in its ascent towards the loftiest aim of all cosmical existence.

The physical in its space aspect is, indeed, the lowest of all, and yet it is the one out of which this charge of narrowness, as made against the Bible and the religious thinking, has most commonly arisen. Since the invention of the telescope, worlds in space, or bodies in space, has been the challenging scientific wonder. It is this which has so greatly weakened, it is said, the old religious belief. It would not be easy to show, however, that even here it had the effect contended for, or that this " opening of the walls of the world," which the science of Lucretius boasted of as loudly as our own, extends greatly beyond what we may call the mere mathematical interest. What real ideas of life, and action, and rationality, and varied orders of being, has it disclosed to us? In all these respects, in answer to all questions prompted by them, the heavens are as silent as of old. The earth is still the centre—the centre of human interest, if not of topical revolution. It is not intended to underrate the ideas thus gained, but they are far from being the greatest. The telescope has revealed to us—what? Distance, number, motion, dynamical relations. This, with some few hints in respect to gases given to us by the spectrum, sums up about all the additions made to our knowledge since the days of Galileo. It has an interest indeed, but of a narrow kind, of a lower rank as compared with those questions of destiny, and of the aim of God's eternal kingdom, for whose solution we are most anxious, and without which other knowledge is a tantalizing darkness, creating at each step more mystery than it explains. Worlds have been discovered—so the term is now used as applied to stellar or planetary bodies; but it is impossible to prove that these worlds, so called, are abodes of life, either in its higher or its lower forms. There are not a few indications to the contrary. There are appearances indicating that a good proportion of these cosmical bodies, whether stellar, planetary, or cometary, are mere wastes in respect to the higher aspects of being. There is no certain knowledge, no probable knowledge of there being in many of them, or in any of them, the very first rudiments of vital organization, any more than in our earth during the millions of ages that geologists assign to its primordial existence, whether gaseous, fluid, or solid. Whewell sets this forth in a remark, whose force strikes us at once: "It is no more incredible," says he, "that there should be *immense space* without life in any of the bodies that occupy it, than that there should be an *immense time* during which one body that we know was in the same azoic condition."

The thoughtful ancient mind regarded the cosmical bodies as being at immense distances, and, therefore, of immense magnitudes, some of them, probably, larger than our earth. There is evidence that the mind went out freely in this expansive direction. The idea was not dependent on any reduction of these distances to decimal numbers, that, beyond a limit by no means great, have only a notional or mathematical interest. In regard to the conceptual greatness nothing is gained by them, since 10,000, or 10,000,000, are equally beyond the conceptive power. Old thinkers, without this, talked even of "the infinity of worlds." With some it was a favorite speculation. "As well think of one head of wheat in a boundless field," says Metrodorus, "as of one world in infinite space." "The *αἴτια*," says Plutarch, "the rational causalities, are infinite, and the effects must correspond;" there was no reason for the one that would not prove the existence of the many. The ancient mind had quite a fair estimate, too, of the *proportional* distances of the planets, though they had no means of bringing them into earthly measurements of miles and inches as deduced from any known earthly parallax. The telescope has helped us here. More perfect instruments, and more perfect observations have given us earthly *base lines*, and we now say it is so many millions of *miles*, and these miles we can bring into feet, and, more wondrous still! even into barleycorns; but the essential knowledge, and the essential reasoning from distance, remain very much the same. The *conceptual* feeling of vastness is not increased by the *notional* estimate. By giving a disproportioned prominence to the mathematical interest, it may be that the emotional has been actually diminished. According to the best evidence of antiquity, Pythagoras held the Copernican system, as it is now called, in its completeness, whilst Plato held it partially. Aristotle, in his book, "De Coelo," condemns it as built upon fanciful or *a priori* reasoning. It placed the sun in the centre, he says, because the fire was the worthier, as it was the more ethereal or heavenly element. This was opposed to observation and sense induction, on which he reasoned as the Bacon of his times. On the Pythagorean system, he maintained, there certainly ought to be an annual parallax of the fixed stars, or some of them. The absence of such parallax, therefore, showed the theory to be false, or else these distances were not merely great, very great, as he held them to be, but inconceivable, vast beyond any measure of computation. We are yet engaged in attempts at solving that problem. I may be permitted to refer to this here, as presenting a singular fact in the history of science and philosophy: The visionary view, the *a priori* view, as the Stagirite calls it, has led to truth, whilst the method of exact science—for Aristotle's argument is founded on legitimate sense induction—landed him and his followers, for many ages, into what is now known to be error. Sense, in its keener instrumental forms, has come at last to support the visionary view. This theory of Pythagoras in respect to the solar system was connected with his other sublime doctrine of the universal harmony, or as he preferred to style it, the music of the spheres. There was grandeur in this outstretching idea, which the telescope is only partially verifying; there was a sublime emotion in it, of more value than any science which lacks it, however exact it may claim to be. And so when David, surveying the nightly heavens, exclaimed: "Lord, what is man?" Or when Isaiah said: "Lift up your eyes on high, and behold all these; who bringeth out their host, who calleth them all by name; it is *because He is strong* that not one of them faileth,"—it is very possible that there may have been a spiritual interest far beyond any that La Place may have felt. To the latter, the heavens were simply his orrery, his diagram for the better exhibition of his mathematical analysis. It shocks all our better thinking to believe that this French atheist had a higher view of the universe, and of the power that rules it than these great religious souls of antiquity, even with their limited knowledge of distance and mathematical relation.

And so, too, in regard to the idea of law, of which we boast as though it were a purely modern thought. They had the substantial knowledge, and that, too, in its purest form. They knew that there must be a cosmical law, even as the cosmos was one. The very name implies unity of organization, and this is the very essence of law. They believed that there was an order in the heavens, in the universal system of things, long before epicycles, or vortices, or gravitation, or correlated forces had been ever heard of: " For ever, O Jehovah, Thy word is settled in the heights;" "all things stand according to Thine ordinance." That there was such a law, a harmony, "making peace in God's high places," a unity in the universe, whatever might be its space extent, this was deemed of higher and more religious value than any knowledge of its numerical details not inspired by this nobler conception. Whether its energy was inversely as the squares, or as the cubes of the distances, or what those distances were in earthly measurements,—of all this they knew but little, even as we know but little more; but they had a transcending knowledge, a far higher thought of it, when they recognized it as *God's law*, God's voice in nature, His Word first uttered in nature's origination, and still sounding on as the security for nature's continuance. Hence they gave it this name so peculiar to the Scritures, but having its shadow in the ancient Greek or Egyptian doctrine of the Logos. What many style law, using it as a wholly impersonal term, denoting no real causal power, but only a series of dead sequences, the Bible calls " The Word of God that runneth very swiftly," pervading as well as sustaining all, and *in which*, as Paul affirms in his echo of this older doctrine (Coloss. i. 15,) τὰ πάντα συνέστηκε, all things consist or stand together. It was but another echo of the old Shemitic thought when Socrates, following Pythagoras, calls it "the harmony that binds together all things in heaven and earth." "He maketh peace in His high places," *concordiam in sublimibus suis.* Cicero but catches the same idea when he says, *orta simul est lex cum mente divina,* which Hooker only translates in that much-lauded utterance of his: "Law has its seat in the bosom of God." Modern thought has enlarged our conception of the universe, it is said; but how is this done? It is by making matter first, the nebula first, the lowest first, and law, love, and reason, all its junior products. Aristotle reverses this. Τὸ καλόν τὸ ἀγαθόν, τὸ νοητόν, the Fair, the Good, the Idea, they are first; they, through νοῦς, mind, or intelligence, move Love, as Love is the great mover of all : κινεῖ δὲ ὡς ἐρώμενον, "*it moves it as being loved.*" * This remarkable declaration, which

---

* "He moves it as being loved." Cudworth following Proclus in his commentary, gives a wrong rendering of this, making it too imaginative, or Platonic, as some would call it. He refers the participle ἐρώμενον to Deity, or the mover, instead of the cosmos. It is the world, or the created " Soul

might have been expected from the semi-poetical Plato, moves our wonder as proceeding from this pure, unimaginative, passionless intellectuality. We find it in the xi. book, sec. 7 of his *Metaphysica*, or "Things above nature:" Κινεῖ δὲ ὡς ἐρώμενον. It is in his argument concerning the First Mover and the first moving things; dry, some would call it, but having a beauty in its very terseness. Law is resolved into the higher idea of love: the world moves because it is loved of the First Mover. Its charm, as well

---

of the world," he would represent as "enamoured with the Supreme Mind, and thus, in imitation of it, continually turning round the heavens." It is the love of the cosmos, or its admiration of the "First Fair and First Good," or the world *drawn* rather than *impelled*. This is beautiful, but it is not the idea of the sober Aristotle. It is rather the love of the Mover towards the cosmos, or to its harmonious movement, which is the *first* moving power. Thus, "the Good" (the 'Αγαθόν) is higher in the eternal order of being than Νοῦς, or Intellect. In one sense it is the 'Αγαθόν, the Good that gives being to the intelligible; or as the Sun in Plato's splendid comparison (*Republic*, vi. 58, E) "gives to things not only their visibility, but also their generation, so does that highest thing, *the Good* (in other places called *love*), not only cause the cognoscibility of things, but also their very "essences and beings." (*Intellectual System of the Universe*, Chap. iv., Sec. xxiii.) When carefully studied, however, the ideas of Aristotle and Plato come to the same thing: the first moving ἀρχὴ is not merely something older than matter or force; it is *Love*, or "*the Good*," higher even than *mind* or *idea*.

as its power, is in its conciseness; τὸ ὀρεκτὸν καὶ τὸ νοητὸν κινεῖ οὐ κινούμενον: "The desire and the thought, in other words, Love and Idea, must be the first movers, themselves the product of no preceding motion." Or according to another statement in the same chapter, *mind*, νους, is the mover of the physical world; but νοῦς may be said to be moved by νοητόν, *mens by intellectum*, mind by truth. Here he stops, but the next step would have carried him to the "Principium," in whom mind and truth, ideal truth, eternal truth, which we cannot think of either as non-existent or as separate from a personal mind, are one and the same. This is the *Primum Movens*, the Logos that was with God and was God. But as it stands, Aristotle's argument is irrefragable: Love is the First Born in the eternal generation he describes. Love and Idea, the Good, and Mind eternally beholding it, are above all motion. They are causes, not effects.

In another chapter (xiii. 4) he reasons, in a similar manner, against those old materialists who maintained that the most imperfect of all things was first, even as their modern brethren do in their nebular theory; in other words, mindless matter first,—force, the force of nothing, first,—contingency first; and then, as things went on (I am giving his very language in his account of these old atheists) προελθούσης τῆς τῶν ὄντων φύσεως, the good and fair, mind and idea, did *somehow* appear." He charges them with bringing more out of less, which is the same as something out of nothing, and compares them with the mythologizers who made Night and Erebus the source of all things, from whom are born both gods and men.

But in regard to that lower conception, the space magnitude, or space relations, or dynamical importance of bodies in the universe, it is all idle to say that these old minds simply conceived of the stars as glow-worm points of light twinkling uselessly in a solid firmament, or sky, just above their heads. Solomon's sublime prayer, "The heaven and heaven of heavens cannot contain thee, cannot *bear* thee," as the Hebrew expresses it, presents a conception transcending anything derived from the modern astronomy as given in our books. David's exclamation shows that he connected the heavenly bodies with ideas vastly transcending man's lowly earthly condition. Without this the sublime rapture becomes inexplicable. Of the stars as bodies inhabited, just as our earth is inhabited, these old worshipers may not have thought. Such an idea is, indeed, found in the Greek poetry, and it may or may not have been in the Hebrew mind. There is no proof to the contrary, as there is no irrationality in the thought that it may have occurred to many a meditative soul in the earlier times. It is still but an *imagination* with us, and there was much to excite the same imagination even before science had got an earthly unit of measurement. There is other proof besides the writings of Aristotle that the ancient men, oriental and occidental, regarded the heavenly bodies as being of immense magnitude, and at incalculable distances. This, however, is quite clear, that they connected with the stars most mighty and glorious existences. "One star differed from another star in glory," but each represented a transcending power in the kingdom of God. It was itself the outshining of an exalted being, or the abode of an exalted being; and there is as much grandeur in that idea, giving as high a conception of the greatness of the universe as would come from the thought of a vast numerical population, whether of mollusks, mastodons, or giants. They were "the Hosts of Heaven," and hence that sublime epithet Jehovah Tsebaoth used in reference to *space* and *rank*, as *Melek Olamim*, King of the Eternities, was employed to denote the *time* aspect of God's kingdom. These mighty stellar powers might have infinite diversity, spiritual as well as dynamic, whereas the modern idea seems tending to an infinite sameness. Our space worlds are but endless repetitions. It is supposed, and that, too, by a fair analogy, that they grow as our earth has grown, and that vast numbers of them are now passing through the same chaotic, life-lacking stages. Seldom do we meet with the thought, as expressed in the scientific world, that any of them have got above us. To science in general man is the *être suprême*. Through him the world is just coming into consciousness. The same conclusions some are deriving from the spectrum; the same gases, the same elementary substances, lead to the idea of sameness in material organization, and this to that of sameness of life in its successive stages—like the earlier inhabitants of our earth as adapted to similar conditions. In this limited scientific space conception of being, repetition is a predominant idea. It suggests a level plane without any towering superiorities, or it resolves itself into an endless succession of material facts, forming a series having eventually no other variations than those of space, numerical quantity, forces, motions, mathematically diversified positions, and relations of atoms. In a word, motion and force, if the two ideas can be separated; these are the only things, *res*, realities. If we want to get any other sounds from this flat, tuneless homophony, we must look elsewhere. We must go to Scripture, or call in the aid of some higher ideas, the seeds of which we may find in our own souls. Science gives no evidence of spiritual dignities. With some it is even a boast that she does not find them.

Which of these two views of the stellar inhabitation or domination is the true one need not be here inquired; nor, should the inquiry be made, could science give us any answer. What has been said has reference only to this claim of grandeur and enlargement, or this common charge that the religious idea of the universe, as derived from the Scriptures, is a narrowing of the human mind. But more of this elsewhere.

The second head of this trine division of the universe, or what I have called its *time* aspect, belongs, in the main, to another lecture; but there are some suggestions in relation to it that connect themselves with the train of thought in which I have here indulged. There is a view of the Biblical creative chronology to which this charge of narrowness may be thought to have some application. It is that which regards not only the tellurian, but the whole cosmical evolution, as the work of one week, or six solar days of our present reckoning, with an infinite blank preceding. A view very different from this, or one that regarded the times as immeasurable, and even ineffable, was held by the best thought of the Church very long before geology as a science was ever heard of. The mediæval doctrine of the cosmos was, in truth, a narrowing from the wider science of the classical world, and from the largeness, moreover, and freedom of earlier patristic interpretations of the Bible. Geographical knowledge, too, had actually sunk within smaller limits, and the discoverer of America but revived cosmical and tellurian ideas which were familiar to some of the freer and bolder thinkers of antiquity, such as Pythagoras, Aristotle, Eratosthenes, Ptolemy, and Pliny. During these mediæval times there had come in more of the thaumaturgic spirit, and the mechanical idea of creation, instantaneously, or almost instantaneously, out of nothing — not only as respects the primal force or matter, but the separate parts and products of the great structure—became a favorite one. It may be said, too, that it was more taken up with the theological *fact* of creation than with the manner or idea. God made the world; in a religious point of view that was all they sought or cared to know. The divine power, the divine command, the idea of instantaneousness, or of very brief times, were dwelt upon as having more of this wonder-working aspect, which the spirit of the times regarded as more closely allied to the religious feeling. This blinded the mind to those other time ideas of birth, growth, succession, evolution, bringing forth, one thing coming out of another,—in a word, of תולדות, "generations," natures, genesis, which to one who now reads the sublime Biblical account, under the influence of a different thinking, appear so prominent that the wonder is they should have been so overlooked. Now there is no need of shrinking from the admission that the change of the current thought in this respect may be attributed, in a good degree, to the influence of modern science; though there never was a time when such an interpretation as that of Saint Augustine would have been deemed heretical. He held it, and others held it in his day, as they have since, for an interpretation having good exegetical grounds in the letter and spirit of the account. No science forced them to it. They found ample support for the idea of extraordinary times in the remarkable language of the Scriptures, and in the peculiar style they employ in setting forth the great facts, in themselves so ineffable, of origin and eschatology.

Revelation is sometimes degraded by attempts to which there is given the sounding name of "reconciliations between religion and science." They are too apt to make science, or what assumes to be such, the constant, and the Bible the variable quantity in the equation. The Scriptures must conform, or they must be made to conform. It is not a work of fair exegesis, but of possible accommodation. It is enough, for example, that any utterly unproved hypothesis denies a distinct beginning of the human species, anything by way of organization or inspiration, anything in the physical, or the spiritual, constituting a specific difference, and making that to be *homo* which before was not *homo*. Such a sweeping conclusion in respect to divine possibilities is taken, at once, as "established science," and straightway some prepare themselves to meet the case by the theory of an ideal Adam. This will do, perhaps, until another demand is made in the name of science, and that is met in an equally prompt and easy way by the theory of an ideal Christ, an ideal incarnation. Scripture shakes hands with science. It is reconciled, as the saying is, and this feat is accomplished by going into the very *interiora* of the Christian creed, and making the Second Adam as unreal as the First. Thus we have our Bibles and science too. We can laud both on the same platform, and this is great gain. We say it boldly:

better reverentially bury the old book than treat it in this way. The boldest denial of infidelity is not more insulting than such a deferential mockery. New facts, in seeming conflict, from well-ascertained history, or well-established science, may set us to re-examine former interpretations, or former applications of them; but we must have an honest faith or none at all. A purely mythical view of the creative account is better than any scientific forcing it will not bear.

There is no science in the Bible, either in its language, its style, or its assumed teaching. Attempts to find it in the artless subjectiveness of its truthful holy writers only leads to delusion. The language of these seers of ineffable things is grounded on their modes of conceiving; their conceptions are shaped by the knowledge of their day. It is their true inspiration that takes this language, and these conceptions, as the best representatives of facts and ideas lying back of all, and which the dialect of science and philosophy fails to reach as much as the vulgar thinking. In truth, nothing shows more strongly the fact of some divine supervision of the Bible, than the absence of any such scientific or philosophic language, or of a style assuming to be that of any special thinking, or of anything esoteric,

THE COSMICAL ARGUMENT. 127

such as has characterized those who have assumed to be religious teachers in all ages. This is wholly lacking even in cases where there would seem to have been the strongest temptation to such a mode of speech. A divine wisdom is here. The scientific or philosophic language of one age is different from that of another. No scientist would dare to say that our own had reached a finality. It may appear even childish a thousand years hence. Now something has kept the Scriptural writers from thus compromising the wondrous book of which, through the ages, they have been the human media of transmission.

In its account of the ineffable truths of origin, the language of the Bible is optical, phenomenal, the vehicle of first appearances. It is a universal language addressed to the most unchanging of the human faculties. Its outside symbols, the same for all ages, represent the ineffable facts, the interior causalities, the ultimate causalities, that lie behind the phenomenal at whatever distance. The speech of science can do no more. It sounds out a mile or two farther from the shore of the directly seen. It brings out a few more interior appearances, but they are still appearances, φαινόμενα, having ever some things yet more interior *of which they are appearances.* The difference is that the Scriptures, in such cases, take the first phenomena, the most visible outward of "the things seen," as the immediate representatives of the deep unseen, whether near, or far off, or even infinitely remote. It names them from such unchanging outlying appearances. Thus there is no pretense of being near the mysterious ultimate causation—such a pretense as science sometimes makes, though still "far wide," still holding on to something they call a *cause*, but which the next increase of the magnifying power turns again into a phenomenon—an *appearance* of something farther back, and still farther back, that appears through it. Thus do they ever verify the deep idea of inspiration, that "the things which are seen are made from things unseen," from causalities that lie, and must for ever lie, beyond the reach of sense, or any science founded on sense. From this never-finished process of turning supposed causalities into new appearances, the dialect of science must be ever becoming obsolete. But the Scripture never commits itself to any mode of speech that must change with changing knowledge of these nearer phenomena; and this is a striking difference between the Bible and other books called sacred. The Koran fails here. It evidently affects sometimes a scientific language, or supposed to be such; as when Mohammed, or his commentators, give the exact number of the heavens, and even the distances, in miles, between them. Something of the same kind may be traced in the oldest books of all other religions, such as the Hindoo, the Persian, and the Chinese. There are appearances of attempts, however crude, at something like scientific theory—feeble efforts at a sort of philosophising, or the utterance of something seemingly above the common mind, an assumption of some esoteric wisdom, or a pretentious teaching style as of persons initiated into mysteries above the ordinary intelligence. There is nothing like this in the Bible. In that book all human thought is put upon a level. From beginning to end, the Scriptures go on their majestic way, manifesting everywhere this strange unconsciousness. There is nothing of the thaumaturgic, or the wonder-making, even when narrating the greatest wonders. When telling of God's descent in the awful flames of Sinai, or of the song of the angels at the Redeemer's birth, they are as calm and unpretending as when narrating the pastoral life of Jacob, or the friendship of David and Jonathan. The Bible never calls attention to the grand things it is saying, or going to say. There is, in style, nothing legendary or sensational about it. It nowhere stops, or stoops, to remove objections; it never betrays any anticipation of cavils. Its perfect subjective truthfulness; when this is understood, the right-minded reader finds it so difficult to resist the evidence of its objective credibility. So honest, so pure, so true within, it cannot be false without.

Thus the Bible never commits itself to any compromising language. It speaks of the heavens in the plural, as it does of eternities in the plural; but it does not number them as the Mohammedans and some of the Jewish Rabbins and Talmudists have done. It speaks of the third heavens, indeed, but only as the symbol of the ineffable space-transcending glory. It has its "heaven of heavens," like its olam of olams, or world of worlds, its all-comprehending sphere, its all-containing time. It leaves these as ever expanding ideas, capable of holding any conceptional content that any science may ever put into them. We may attempt to make it more scientific by describing these plural heavens as atmospherical, astronomical, planetary, stellar, nebular, but all this never exhausts the Scriptural language. It takes in something beyond all physical worlds which, in their widest extent, are but the lowest spheres in the kingdom of

God. It carries the mind to that transcending οὐρανὸς to which "Christ lifted up His eyes" when He said: "And now, Father, glorify thou Me with the glory which I had with Thee before the world was," πρὸ τοῦ τὸν κόσμον εἶναι. The Bible language is not to be limited by the conceptual faculty, whether that of Solomon or of Herschell. It points to the glory which is above the heavens, over the heavens, *super coelos.* It goes up, up, to the throne of God, the eternal seat of the highest power and the highest intelligence, wherever that may be, or in whatever space relations, whether conceived as central, altitudinous, profound, or all-present. "He looketh down to behold the things that are in the heavens, as well as the things that be on the earth." It is a locus all-transcending; it is a language all-satisfying, intelligently guiding the common religious mind, whilst giving a view, if we choose to take it, inexhaustible by science or any amount of inductive knowledge. The Bible statements of origin, its view of the universe in its relation to God—the only view of any spiritual value—so transcends all sense-knowledge that it can never truly come in collision with it, or require reconciliation.

And yet, in saying this, there is not excluded a proper deference to science as suggestive of something in these ever-mounting senses that certain preconceived limitations may have kept us from seeing. We apply this principle of new knowledge expanding, though not contradicting, old language, and we find no difficulty in it when we interpret the earlier Scriptures from the standpoint of a higher theological knowledge derived from the later revelations. Christ and Paul give us a better understanding of Moses and the Prophets. The mind receives an enlargement from the New Testament writings, and we legitimately carry this back to the better interpretation of the Old, discovering thereby " wondrous things out of God's ancient Law." The Pentateuch, the Psalms, the Prophets, yea the history, the genealogy, and the chronology of the Old Testament seem to carry a higher sense. Its devotional assumes a more heavenly, its ethics a more spiritual aspect. That higher sense was, seminally, there before, and some minds of unwonted spirituality had, even then, a glimpse of it. It is not a mere kábala, accommodation, or type even. It is not a double sense, or a mere arbitrary mystical sense. It is a mounting sense, a germinant sense, built firmly, indeed, upon the letter, and rising legitimately from it, but now satisfying, or tending to satisfy, that glow, and warmth, and elevation of diction which before seemed so strange in its connection with facts of a seemingly lower order. David and Pindar both seem to be celebrating temporal victories, temporal deliverances; but what a difference in their styles! What a rising is there in the spiritual emotional as produced by the Hebrew Psalms when we read them in the revealing light of David's greater Son, bringing out the rays that lay latent in the spectrum, or were, in comparison, but dimly seen. It is like the feeling with which the newly-converted soul takes up the whole volume of Scripture. What has changed? The language is the same. The logical significance of words in their logical relations are the same; but how sublimely have they risen in what may be called the scale of spiritual emotion! Though lexically the same, what a glory seems now to invest certain oft-recurring words: God, life, salvation, righteousness, truth, mercy, holiness, forgiveness, the fear of the Lord, the kingdom and people of the Most High, the Anointed One of whom such glories are predicted, but which so shrink when applied to an earthly monarch, or an earthly salvation. "Jehovah reigns, let earth rejoice." Had we ever read that before? But there they stand, the same words as of old before the Psalms became the undying liturgy of the church; but how have they all ascended, not to a different exegetical defining, but to a higher plane of significance. The temporal salvation; how it expands into the greater evangelical idea, not by taking a new sense, strictly, for God's salvation is ever in essence the same, even as the faith that looks to it is ever the same—but by rising up towards that measurement which is indicated by the otherwise inexplicable glow of the language.

This train of thought might be farther pursued. It has, however, been dwelt upon here simply as the basis of another application, not of the same kind, indeed, but suggestive of a similar analogy. If an advance of theological knowledge may, legitimately, have this retrospective effect in our interpretation of the older Scripture, why may not an assured advance in physical knowledge give something of the same legitimate advantage, putting us in a position to see—if it is really God's glory we wish to see—more of vastness in the Scriptural language, a vastness truly there, though veiled by narrowing conceptions as much outside, in their assumed literalness, as the later knowledge that demands conformity? Interpreted from itself it has ample room for both.

For example: the great time ideas had been acknowledged by the best minds of an early age.

The older versions, Greek, Latin, and Syriac, had given them with remarkable fulness. The strange pluralities of the words by which they are set forth appear in the Hebrew with a breadth and power that cannot so well be expressed in our modern, European tongues, in consequence both of the vagueness and of the limitations that have entered into the age-worn corresponding terms. Hence it is that there have been given to such expressions as "eternities," "King of eternities," "kingdom of all eternities," "world of worlds," "ages of ages," "*secula seculorum*," altogether inadequate representatives. This Bible language had become narrowed, too, from other causes, such as the growing cosmical ignorance before alluded to, and the too exclusive predominance of that religious dogma of the naked divine power which favored the instantaneous or mechanical view of creation, and thus threw into the background the mighty significance of some of the chief words entering into the creative account. But when the thoughts of men were turned, though in another way, to the antiquity of the earth, and the evidence of it all around us —as capable of estimate by the common mind, when aroused to it, as by the most scientific— then this sublime Scriptural account of the world's evolution was found to have a vastness felt, indeed, before by the profoundest minds, though lacking the scientific data for reducing it to a definite conception. There was something great, mysterious, immeasurable—no thoughtful man could read the First of Genesis without feeling that—and thus there came easily, or without the sense of forcing, the idea that there must be a correspondence, in the picture, between the great causation and the great effects, the great *evolutions* and the great *times* through which they were divinely evolved. This Scriptural account is most unique. It never grew as myths and legends are known to grow. It is a whole, as it must have presented itself to one mind. The thought, then, suggests itself at once. A narrative of things so wholly out of the way of any human knowledge, direct or traditional, is either a studied invention — a thing very hard to be believed of that age, and of events involving such a religious grandeur of idea— or its claim to credence must be grounded on the alleged fact of some vision revelation. The pictorial style confirms this. It is a painting, and, as such, demands a standpoint and a perspective that shall bring the whole representation into harmony. In rendering easier the attainment of such a pictorial view, science has aided us. It has helped us to appreciate the vast thought that is in the Scriptures with more objective clearness, if not with more subjective fulness of emotion. In taking this vantage ground, we do not hamper ourselves by any deference to outside authority. We explore the Bible anew, but with the feeling that we are not putting upon it a new sense. It is simply getting from this sublime Biblical frontispiece what lies fairly within the scope of its mighty purpose, and the full significance of its most vivid as well as most suggestive language.

LECTURE IV.

COSMICAL ARGUMENT CONTINUED.—WORLDS IN TIME.

LECTURE IV.

COSMICAL ARGUMENT CONTINUED.—WORLDS IN TIME.

The creative account—Six solar days — Creation *in time*—Ideas of growth, succession, evolution—Difficulties of the solar day theory—The word *day*—The *periodical* in distinction from the mere *metaphorical* sense—Language of birth and growth, as patent on the first of Genesis—*Proportion* in times necessary to its conceivability—Feeling of vastness in the creative account—Its exceeding sublimity—Its language to be treated as self-interpreting—The words *darkness, night, light, day,* to be determined from the account itself—The first day determines all the rest—The whole creation called a day—No mention of short days in other parts of Scripture — No absolute measure of time—Ratios alone conceivable—Impression of vastness in other creative descriptions of the Bible, Psalm xc—Mountains *born*—Birth-travail of the earth—Proverbs viii—Leaves an impression of immense antiquity—Job xxxviii—The sea *born*—The Hebrew terms expressive of a struggle of forces—The ungovernable sea—Psalm civ—Summary of Biblical creative ideas—Charge of narrowness against the Scriptures repelled—Stuart and Hitzig on the absence of divided time in the world to come—The view unscriptural—*The Malkuth kol Olamim*, or "kingdom of all eternities"—Æonic words of the New Testament.

THE Bible in its relation to the *space aspect* of the universe was considered in the previous lecture. The *time aspect* in connection with the infidel argument drawn from our later cosmical and geological science, next demands our attention. The Mosaic account of the terrestrial primordia has become one of the principal grounds on which modern scepticism assails the credibility of Revelation. At the same time it has not received from our theologians and commentators that attention which its importance, as an outpost, at least, if not the very citadel of divine truth, so imperatively demands. Its defence has been, in a great degree, left to the mere assertion of the truisms before alluded to, such as the impossibility that the book of nature should contradict the book of inspiration, since God is the author of both; and then the argument that follows is drawn almost wholly from science, or some assumed scheme of agreement, instead of being derived from the Bible itself, or any attempt at an exposition of its wondrous ideas as grounded on fair and careful exegesis.

The theory of six solar days, each of twenty-four hours as now measured by the risings and settings of the sun, is seldom maintained at the present day, whether the Mosaic account is supposed to refer to the terrestrial or to the cosmical creation. This more limited view was the one generally held, and truthfully held, we may say, when the purely religious idea of a divine creation was the one prominently demanded, and there were no outside views pressingly calling attention to the *processes* and the *times*, although it could not have failed to be seen by the thoughtful reader that creation *in time*, creation by order, by evolving successions, generation, birth, growth, was an idea lying on the very face of the letter, and repeated with emphatic variety of diction. Still the length of these *times*, the evolutions implied in this peculiar language of creation, or rather of generation, were, in the main, overlooked as subordinate, or non-essential ideas. It cannot be denied, however, that they drew the attention of some thoughtful minds, and those the greatest known in the early ages of the Church. This has been already alluded to. But the question comes to us for our own exegetical determination: Is there a *time* aspect, a real time aspect, in the creative account? Does the evidence lie upon its very face? Does this temporal idea enter into it as well as those of power and a divine causation? Does the very harmony of this wonderful narrative, the true perspective of this marvelous picture, require that there should be also a true proportion in these times, so as to make it a veritable creation in time, instead of a mere show of it out of analogy with the temporal processes fairly suggested by the generative language employed? There can be no doubt of the ideas that would have arisen in our minds, had no time word been used. The great eventualities, as narrated one after the other, would have resolved themselves into corresponding periods. The "seas gathering," the "land appearing," its surface "drying," the waters "swarming" with life, the earth " bringing forth," the "herb-seeding seed," man making his appearance as the latest evolution of the evoking Word; all this would have associated itself with an harmonious ideal of times and successions, having something of that true proportion without which the events, as events, cannot well be conceived. No language in itself can be more opposed to that idea of mechanical or outside fabrication, which is sometimes ignorantly charged upon the Mosaic account.

Now, does the introduction of the word *day* control all this other peculiar phraseology, or is it to be controlled *by* it, especially in view of its well-known cyclical or periodical idea in all the earliest forms of speech, and still showing its traces in numerous modern idioms? This is the great question for the interpreter, although there are others of equal importance that demand attention in connection with it. Give us room here, if the language allows it. Do there fairly come in the ideas of vastness, of great successions, of mighty evolutions originated by a series of divine fiats? If the picture gives us this, it gives us something more to complete the harmony of its divine perspective. Have we, then, this room? Have we this mighty order from chaos to light, from light to life, from life to humanity,—commencing in darkness, formlessness, and vapor, rising by a succession of most sublime stages, through the vegetable and the animal, up to a world of rational, moral, and spiritual being? Have we this room? Then let science fill up the details of the grand outline according to her means, and at her leisure. There will always be room enough in it for her as well as for the theologian. Whether drawing on fact or fancy, she will always find herself somewhere within the bounds of this roll of development. Even should one succeed, or fancy that he had succeeded, in bringing the Scriptural account, in all its stages, to a perfect agreement with some scientific scheme, without any overlappings or interlappings, or deviations of parallel, it would be of little avail, since there is no knowing how long that scientific language might maintain its stamp, or how long that scientific scheme would last before being superseded by another.

But this is a lecture and not a treatise. Only a few points, therefore, can be presented, and they are all that are necessary for a fair understanding of the whole question, resting, as it does, on certain strong grounds which can be clearly, yet briefly, enumerated. There is,—

1st. The immense difficulty of reconciling the

primordial epochs of creation, as given in Genesis, with the conception of a first day, having its beginning even before the light, and yet made as a day is now made by the rising and setting, or by the setting and rising of the sun. If it be said that we need not suppose those diurnal commencings and endings, and especially that first one of all, to be made as now, but in some other mysterious manner, that would seem like giving up the prime ground of those who have most to say about literal interpretation, or about the word day meaning day, that is, an ordinary solar day, and nothing more. If it is not an ordinary day, then it is an extraordinary day, or a *dies ineffabilis*, as Augustine calls it, and they know not how far this may lead them. Some such idea of ineffability seems to have been in the early Jewish mind in the days of Josephus, if we may judge by what he says of it in the beginning of the first book of his Antiquities. If any choose to introduce the word *mysterious*, they must make more of it. If they talk of unknown hypothetical methods, they should be modest in their denunciations of those whom they charge with profanely departing from the plain letter of the account. The mysterious, the ineffable, are here undoubtedly, but it may be in the very nature of the day, or its ineffable *duration*, as well as in the manner of its phenomenal production. The one is no more an indispensable element of the diurnal idea than the other. A certain duration is no more a fixed component of the notion suggested by the term, than a stated rising and setting of the sun, or some revolution, real or apparent, by which they are produced. The making of such a solar day in the primordial epoch, as described in the account, and giving it its exact length of twenty-four hours, half for the day and half for the mysterious night that precedes, is a difficulty not created by science, not to be cured by it. It is patent on the very face of the account, if we would make it consistent with itself, and it must have been as evident to the early unscientific mind to whom the vision was first given, and by whom it was first narrated, as it is to us. In his ecstatic vision, he sees no sun rising over the dark waters of the *tehom*, but he hears a voice saying, " Let there be light," and a light shines out of the chaos, and upon the chaos; formlessness gives way to form and visibility; and this is the morning of his first day.

Our second ground of reasoning is the *periodical* sense of the word *day*, and especially as it is used in the early languages, classical and Shemitic. Closely connected with this is the sense of day as a completed time, or the epochal idea, as it may be called:

"Longa dies perfecto temporis orbe."

This epochal sense is a very different thing from the *metaphorical*, with which some would confound it, and which, by itself, would furnish a very weak support for so grave an argument. Tropical or metaphorical would denote merely a *metaphora*, or *transfer* to another form of thought, presenting merely an analogy of cause, effect, or incidental resemblance. Day, however, as epoch or cycle, carries with it the essential idea of completed period with its completed work. It is a rounded course, determined not by mere duration, however measured, but by an order of movement having its proper commencement and ending as made by two contrasted states, as of rest and progress, torpor and movement, death and life, birth and growth, appearance and disappearance, light and darkness, or evening and morning—the one the privation or minimum, the maximum or complement, of the other. Any one such application of the word day, *dies*, *yom*, to any completed cyclical ordo, is no more metaphorical than any other. Of such a time period the solar day is to us the nearest, shortest, and most visible representative. Hence it easily enters language as its readiest denominator. Thus *day* is used for ordo, period, series of events, longer or shorter, whilst year is rarely, generation more frequently, but week, month, century, never employed for any such purpose. The language, then, is not arbitrary, nor metaphorical, nor depending on the fancy, but has a law determining the class of ideas to which it is applied. Hence *dies* in Latin is used for the period of human life, as ἡμερα in Greek is sometimes synonymous with αιων, or *age*, used in the same way—the period of existence, life with its evening and morning, its coming out of darkness, and its emergence into light—*venire in diem*, as the Romans said. That we are not forcing things here is shown by the undeniable fact, that this cyclical idea is attached to the word *yom* in the second chapter, where it most unmistakably represents the whole process, or rounded period of creation, whether regarded as tellurian or cosmical. It is all one day from the primordial chaos up to man: "These are the generations of the earth and heavens, in the *day* the Lord created them"—in their being created. The Hebrew is exegetical: בהבראם, "in the process called their being created"—the infinitive in this case being more pictorial than any noun representing simply the fact or event

of creation could possibly have been. "*Before
the day*" was, or "*from* the day" I am HE. Isaiah
xliii. 13. The day of the prophet must be the
great day mentioned here—*dies longissima perfecto
tempores orbe*. It immediately suggests to us the
ἡμέραν αἰῶνος, the æonic day, or the day of eternity,
as the language is used. II. Peter iii. 18. We
also think of the last great day of which the
Scripture so solemnly speaks, that "consummation of the ages, συντέλεια τῶν αἰώνων, that rounded
series of events, be it longer or shorter, when the
closing physical changes shall take place, or the
present mundane system shall be wound up as
preparatory to a new day of creation still more
complete and glorious. The language of the
Scriptural protology is simply parallel to that
of its eschatology; and there should be no hesi-
tation in applying the same mode of exegesis in
the one case that we so readily admit in the
other. It might seem like marring the artless
grandeur of this old language to admit the
thought of anything studied, and yet it does look
as though the writer had been led to use this remarkable expression of *day* as applied to the
whole series, to prevent mistake in its application
to the six divisions, or as a key to its wider significance, when the course of knowledge should

prepare the way for its more easy, but not less natural reception.

The third thing demanding attention presents itself in the words before alluded to as denoting growth, succession, evolving, or one thing coming out of another, birth, generation; in a word, all that is meant by *nature*, φύσις, תּוֹלְדוֹת, in the old languages, and their direct derivatives in the modern; the very name Genesis, as coming from the Greek Septuagint version, being suggestive of this whole class of ideas; since ἡ βίβλος γενέσεως, the book of Genesis, or Generation, is but a translation of the Hebrew אֵלֶּה תּוֹלְדוֹת: "These are the generations of the heavens and the earth." The wonder is that such a kind of language should have been so overlooked. There they are, these words of birth and evolution, and they are not mere meaningless expletives to be shrivelled up in their wide significance, by being all made dependent on the contracted notion we attach to the single word of time. There must be proportion in the chronology, or the time idea, so essential an element in the account, cannot keep the emphasis its importance so evidently demands. Now, in determining the proportion, there is no exegetical reason why the word *day* should overrule the force of all these significant terms, rather than that itself should be interpreted by them. Without it these other words become wholly arbitrary, empty of any available meaning or application—in short, utterly unthinkable. It could not have been meant that there was a real "*growth*" and "*birth*," a real "bringing forth," a real "seeding seed," as by some real causation passing through all its stages, and yet that the cedar of Lebanon, from the quickening of its root-germ in the earth to the waving of the topmost branch of its lofty height, was produced in the same time, or, rather, in an hour or so of the same time, with "the hyssop that groweth out of the wall." To instantaneous production, reason could have made no objection. As a divine fact, had it been so revealed, no science could deny its possibility. But the other supposed mode, or that of great evolutions in inconceivably disproportionate times, or bearing no analogy to the relations of parts thus evolved, is delusive, magical, inconceivable, unthinkable. The language suggests a process, generative and physical, and yet that process lacking the element of ratio, without which it cannot, as a process, be made an object of thought at all. We cannot conceive of growth, or the passing of an organism from one stage to another, except as a passage through every intervening point, and in proportionate times. The crowding, therefore, of processes so immensely different into times having so little of a corresponding ratio, has all the difficulty of instantaneousness, without its grandeur and its conceivable rationality as the product of almighty power.

This disturbance of the conceptive faculty comes from the assumption of the short solar day of a few hours, so apparently conflicting with the other no less marked and unmistakable language of birth, succession, evolution. Which is to control? Is the single time word to be so interpreted as to take all meaning out of the others? This would be all the more strange, when we bear in mind that that same word is plainly used for the whole great process of creation, from its primordial amorphic state, until it ends in the Sabbath and in humanity. What right has any one to call such reasoning far-fetched, or to regard it as putting a force upon the language of Scripture?

The fourth thing to be noticed in this summary of an argument is the aspect of vastness—I can use no better term—which gives its sublime effect to this whole Mosaic account, and especially to its beginning. It is somehow felt by a thoughtful mind, even when acquiescing in that twenty-four hour day view, which nothing from without has as yet disturbed. Vast power, vast bodies, vast forces, vast movements, vast changes, vast causations, vast effects! There comes along with it the feeling of vast time. A feeling we have called it, for such it is even before it assumes the form of a distinct exegetical idea. It was this which so affected the mind of Augustine, and led him to characterize these times as "*dies ineffabiles*," days unspeakable, either as immense evolutions, *morae,* "*delays*" in nature, as he sometimes calls them, suspensions, or as transcending the idea of time altogether. It is this, too, which makes the vision theory of the creative revelation so acceptable, as giving a relieving *perspective,* carrying what may really seem short, and is short, as measured on the canvas, to the vast proportion required for the pictorial harmony. This may not be the experience of all in the study of the passage, but it becomes very strong and vivid when a contemplative mind, divesting itself of all prepossessions, and giving full admission to this sense of grandeur, regards the account as *sui generis,* self-interpreting, defining its own terms from the very nature of the ideas presented. Thus read, this impression of vastness comes in so naturally, that it affects our sense of the times. The panorama so spreads out before us; the dark abyss of waters, the breaking light, that first mysterious evening of the formless chaos, the morning, the separation, the naming, the evoking Word—all is so great, so sublime, on the vaster scale, that the forcing, if there be any, appears wholly in the narrowing interpretation. Am I overstating this? Where in ancient or in modern literature can there be found a page of such superhuman grandeur of conception, of such soul-awing majesty of diction as this: "In the beginning God created the heavens and the earth. And earth was formless and void, and there was darkness on the face of the deep. And the breath of Elohim was brooding on the face of the waters. And God said, Let it be light, and there was light. And God saw the light that it was good. And God divided between the darkness and between the light; and the light called He day, and the darkness called He night; and there was an evening, and there was a morning—day one." The last clause is plainly exegetical, or explanatory of what precedes. It tells us what this night and morning were. It explains this mystery of a day not measured by the sun, but having an ineffable division of its own : And *thus* was there an evening, and *thus* there was a morning—day one. The process itself defines them in its two great evolving stages : And *thus* there was a night, and *thus* there was a day, making, so far as this Mosaic account is concerned, the primordial time in the earth's greater chronology. To interpret this rightly, look not abroad. Keep to the record, and you will find its meaning there. There can be clearly traced all the ideas corresponding to the mighty words—the night, the day, the evening, the morning, for which you are seeking. The account is self-interpreting. What was that primeval night which comes first in this creative movement, as it does in all traditional derivations? The answer is most distinct. It was the darkness that was resting on the face of the deep—the void and formless *tehom*. How long had it been thus resting? No answer is returned from the silence. To get twelve hours here before the light, to find any rule for their measurement, their commencement, or their separation from anything preceding—to do this is the forcing, as I have elsewhere shown, and shall not therefore dwell upon it in this rapid summary. And where is the morning? Once more we interrogate the oracular language. The answer comes again with unmistakable clearness: It was the light which the divine Word evolved from the darkness—the light that shone not only *on* the darkness, but "out of the darkness," ἐκ τοῦ σκότους, as the Apostle understands it. These two events make the chronological day, the primeval period with its own peculiar work and history separate from all others. It is God himself who names and defines them, whatever may be the import of that mysterious language. HE gives us our lexicon here: And the darkness He called night, and the light called He *day*—and thus there was an evening, and thus there was a morning—day one. We get a reason for the strange repetition of that solemn heraldic formula, taking away all its seeming tautology. Why so often said, and with such a proclamatory sameness, unless to call attention to something extraordinary in the mornings and evenings so announced? The view taken is drawn fairly from the language arousing wonder like the similar heraldic announcements of the seals and trumpets in the Revelations. But now attempt to force in the measurement of twenty-four hours, and what a collapse of grandeur, what a derangement of proportion seems immediately to take place. I have dwelt upon this, because anxious to give the impression so strong and clear to my own mind, that these ideas of vastness come directly from the face of the account, as read in its own clear light, and are not forced upon it by any outside pressure. An interpretation thus pressed upon us from without undermines faith instead of affording any sure foundation. We use with confidence the language of Augustine: "These are God-named times, God-divided times." There is a vastness in the language, an infinite suggestiveness compared with which, so far as sublimity is concerned, the geological decimals are utterly frigid and unemotional. The mind is not narrowed in believing the Mosaic record of creation.

The first great day determines all the rest. They all have the mark of this higher chronology. They were all divine evolutions. In each of them the old chaotic darkness and formlessness more and more disappear. New mornings break forth, "shining clearer and clearer unto the perfect day," when humanity, as it had been physically evolving out of the dust of all below, becomes complete in the *primus homo*, made such by the inspiration of God, and set forth as the type of a new and higher order of being. Here is no forcing. It is a view that comes from the very spirit of the sublime passage, breathing through every mysterious word, and filling the soul of the devout reader with a feeling of its truthfulness, as well as of its glory. It requires no scientific hypothesis. It transcends science. It needs no "reconciliation;" for it stands out of the reach of all collision.

In the fifth place I would briefly call attention to this aspect of vastness, these ideas of great time successions, as they appear in other parts of the Bible. They have, indeed, a poetical character, but this strengthens the argument. It was this very aspect on which I am insisting that made the creative times such a grand subject for poetry, and called out, in relation to them, such a poetical pictorialness. And here is to be noticed, in the first place, a fact that demands special attention. It is the absence, from all other parts of the Scriptures of any allusion to these brief days as such, or as being solar in their character. The Fourth Commandment forms no real exception to this remark; since it is simply a repetition of the earlier language, carrying with it the same scale of interpretation, and confirming it by the undeniable difference that must be admitted between the divine and human days, if we would preserve at all the analogous parallel between the human work, the human rest, on the one hand, the ineffable divine work, and the ineffable divine rest on the other. There is no longer type and antitype, no temporal sign of the Æonian Sabbath, when both are reduced to the same measurement. Now in all the other passages which are not repetitions but vivid descriptions drawn from this original picture, the brief solar day, had it been really conceived as such, would have been the most memorable, the most likely to be recalled, of all the features of the account. It would have been the great wonder, had the Hebrew mind truly received from it such an idea of chronological brevity. But no such feeling anywhere shows itself. In some places we have what seems to be a representation of instantaneousness: "He spake and it *was*, He commanded and it *stood;*" but that refers to the divine Word, or Fiat, as accomplished in its very utterance—"the Word running very swiftly," to use the language of the Psalmist, or as a very early apocryphal writer interprets it, ὁ λόγος διήκων πάσης κινήσεως κινητικώτερος, "the pervading Word having a more rapid movement than all motion;" to us, indeed, the slow course of nature and the ages, to God, swifter than any electric current. To the divine mind all effects must be patent in their causes, whether natural or supernatural, and so the first, which is this outgoing Word, is the veritable fulfilment of the remotest sequence. This is shown in that solemn formula so oft repeated in Genesis, וַיְהִי כֵן, "and it was so," it stood firm; the nature commenced by the fiat had in it all that should be evolved until that seminal force was spent, or had prepared the way designed for a new evolution. But we know from the account itself, that neither in respect to the universal or any partial development, was it instantaneous. It was a creation *in time*. Such is a prominent idea of the representation. Was it real or seeming? Had it relative proportion in its parts? For of time, irrespective of its ratios, we have no more any absolute measure than we have of space. It is an axiom of Newton that the space worlds might all exist within the compass of what we call an inch, and yet every ratio perfectly maintained as now existing between the parts. We are forced to admit the same of time. The earthly history might all lie within the extent of a minute, and yet with a perfect proportion in every measure of its eventualities. Thus regarded, rapidity of growth is wholly relative, though still *growth* in the truest sense of the word. We have something like this before our very eyes. In the few weeks' incubation of the egg there is a series of transformations, without leap or discontinuance, a transition through every stage, and with as many eventualities as Darwin's imagination finds in the ages intervening between a portion of the mundane egg of the nebulous fluid and the perfect species as it now exists. Till science can explain this, it should be more modest in its claims to understand the secret of life and the origin of worlds. In fact, time absolute, having no relation to other times, is inconceivable. It is ratio that makes its rationality as an object of thought. With it, time properly begins. Proportion is demanded, or the ideas of birth, growth, order, succession—in a word, of genesis or generation,—become wholly illusory. Without it, it is not succession,—the succession of causality; it is not order; it is not natural; it is not supernatural, originating nature and working in it. It is contranatural, unnatural, out of all order, out of all analogy. It lacks alike the grandeur of instantaneousness, and the reasonableness of a proportional evolution. The language employed in Genesis would not have been used for a causality which is neither timeless, nor having the proportions which a real chronology demands.

We see this in studying those other passages in the Bible of which creation forms the theme. There is nowhere in them any allusion to this wonder of time suspension, as in the miracles of Joshua and Hezekiah. A far greater marvel would it have been, far more likely to enter into the thought and demand the attention, had such time brevities, or time suspensions, been really regarded as belonging to the story of creation, and as characterising its great eventualities. What a mighty series! Light evolving from a primeval chaos, waters dividing, an atmospherical firmament uprising, seas gathering to their beds, oceans subsiding, lands upheaving, the dry soil appearing, coming into view, *making itself visible*, as the pictorial Hebrew gives it by an optical deponent verb so suggestive of gradualness—the waters teeming with life of every kind from the infusoria to the *tanninim*, or great monsters of the deep—the ground *bringing forth* from the fungus to the oak—the celestial bodies beginning their time divisions—man at last derived in some way from the previous elements of nature, his physical thus coming from the dust, "first of the earth earthly," then inspired by God, separated from nature by the divine image, raised above nature—in an ineffable manner constituted a sexual duality—invested with the dominion of the world—wonders like these, evolutions like these, and all taking place between sun and sun of a 24-hour solar-day—a creation in time indeed, and that makes it the greater wonder, but without the proportions which such an immense diversity of works would demand in a real causal or time process wherein the parts bore a due relation, to say the least, to each other! Now this might have been. Our argument is not now to be understood as contending against the possibility of such a series of events in themselves considered, or the credibility of such a time hastening, or time suspension. It is the exceeding improbability, the inconceivability, I might almost say, of the fact, that such a wonderful disproportion between the times and the successions so graphically set forth should have actually been in the thought of the Psalmist, and other Scriptural writers who dwell upon the creative scenes, and yet without the least mention of it, though forming, as it would have done, the great marvel of the account.

Are we not justified, then, in the conclusion that the creative account, of which the poetical writers of the Bible are so full, did not so present itself to the old Hebrew mind? The fact is most significant in respect to the earliest interpretations of this most ancient document.

In proof, let me first refer especially to Ps. xc., civ., Prov. viii., and Job xxxviii. From all these we derive a peculiar impression. It is that same feeling of vastness by which we are affected in reading the narrative in Genesis; vastness of power, vastness of event, vastness of time, all alike transcending measurement. Now, from none of these later pictures, if studied by themselves, would such an idea of solar days, or of comparatively brief time successions, have ever been obtained. In all of them the idea of great evolutions in correspondent times is strikingly suggested, as it is also in the Persian cosmogony, evidently a copy of this old painting, but in which "*six times*" appear as the translation of the "six days." It may be referred to as one of the strongest proofs in respect to that oldest understanding of this matter which is now said to have been forced upon us by modern science. In the Biblical passages referred to, if we regard them as standing by themselves, there is nothing to interfere with the largest exegesis. The great ideas, the תולדות, generations, evolutions, coming out of one thing, or of one state of things, from another, appear everywhere, both descriptively and etymologically. They present vividly every conception of the old account except that of the brief day. I have already remarked on that early title as given in the beginning of Gen. ii., "the generations of the heavens and the earth." The language of Job and the Psalms might be regarded as a commentary, or even as a translation. So the Greek title before alluded to, βίβλος γενέσεως, the book of *Genesis*, has something about it most significant. There can hardly be a doubt that this name, and the other generative terms sounding then in the near vernacular of the Septuagint version, did exert an influence on the early Greek Church, and especially on men like Origen and Clement, in predisposing them to the wider interpretation of times and causalties. The very word *Genesis*, although it is an exact representative of the Hebrew תּוֹלְדָה, was unfavorable to any idea of arbitrary or mechanical fabrication. Had that name been given to our English version: "*The Book of Generations*"—the generations of the earth and heavens—it is not too much to say that it would have greatly modified the common thinking on this great subject.

The language of the XC. Psalm has an unmistakable reference to the creative and anti-creative times. The allusion is not simply to ancient historical times on earth, to which the olamic or æonian words are sometimes applied; for it was at a period before "the hills were born," that God existed, מֵעוֹלָם וְעַד עוֹלָם, from Olam to Olam, ἀπὸ τοῦ αἰῶνος καὶ ἕως τοῦ αἰῶνος, *a sæculo in sæculum*, "from world to world." Before the mountains were *born*: It is the passive of the verbal root of the noun תּוֹלְדוֹת, rendered *generations*. Poetical, it may be said, but we have Aristotle's authority for holding that poetry may be most closely allied to philosophy. We know, too, that from early vivid metaphors philosophy draws its most impressive language, however fossilized it may become in its later abstractedness. "Before the mountains were *born*—we put the emphasis on this word—before thou hadst *formed* the earth or the world": The translation of the second clause is inadequate, and too suggestive of bare mechanical or outside fabrication. The verb employed is wholly and strikingly generative, and the idea of formation it denotes must correspond to it.* It is a term used to describe the pangs of child-birth, from the primary significance of twisting, thence writhing, struggle, *torture*, just as the latter word comes from the Latin word torqueo. Hence, in the next stage, it becomes a general term for parturition, from which the translation is direct to that of production, or physical birth. But the writhing, struggling, agonizing sense ever adheres to it in all its applications. It is production with labor, with overcoming strength ex-

---

* Had the word employed been the more outward or seemingly mechanical term of *formation*, like יָצַר or עָשָׂה, the idea would have been the same, though less vividly expressed. For Scripture sometimes seems to reverse its language : "Before I formed thee," (*fashioned*, וְיָצָרְךָ), it was said of Jeremiah. Here an undoubted *generative* process is represented as a *direct* work. So the "*possessing* the reins," the "overshadowing in the womb," (the *quickening*), and the "*fashioning* of the members," in Psalm cxxxix.

erted against resisting forces. The old Greek and Latin translators read the Hebrew word without vowels, and regarded it as passive, with the third person feminine preformative instead of the second person masculine. Hence they rendered: "before were formed or generated, γεννηθῆναι, the earth and the world." The Syriac makes "earth" the subject, and yet renders it actively: "Before earth travailed in the birth," keeping up the same figure that is used in respect to the mountains. With the established Masoretic punctuation, the only maintainable rendering is that which takes it as active, with Deity for the subject, and yet giving it the common travailing or parturitive sense: "Before the mountains were born, yea, before thou didst travail in birth with the earth or the world, from olam to olam, from eternity to eternity, art thou, O God." It is an awful figure; the anthropopathism is, indeed, a most bold and startling one;* but a tremendous idea was demanding ut-

---

* By giving the verb here the passive punctuation, and regarding "earth" as the subject, taken in the feminine, we avoid the anthropopathism that some might deem offensive: "*Before the earth travailed in the throes of parturition.*" But it is the same great idea of immense forces struggling in the womb of generation. The boldest rendering, however, is not only the most grammatical, but most clearly in the style of Scripture. So God's love is compared to a mother's yearning

terance, and the soul of the prophet, the "Man of God," as he is called in the title of this very old psalm, was laboring to bring it forth. It is the birth travail in the production of the world, and that, strange as the thought may appear, ascribed to Deity! If it is an "accommodation," as some would call it, an aid to our effort at conceiving the ineffable, then let us be humbly accommodated by it:

> Before the hills were born, or earth
> The throes of life had known,
> From world to world, art thou, O God;
> Immovable Thy throne.

For emotional grandeur; for the feeling that comes from the "Living Word," and without which thought and knowledge are dead, what are meiocene, and pleiocene, and eocene, and the frigid decimals of the geological notation to the power of language like this? There is, too, an awful suggestiveness in the figure. It brings up

---

affection for her offspring. Isaiah xlix. 15. There is the same startling figure in Deut. xxxii. 18: "The Rock that begat thee, the God that *bare* thee." In the second clause it is the participle of this same verb (*meholel*), and there is the same idea of *difficulty*, God's travailing, as in the birth, with the rebellious and refractory Israel, requiring the strongest resources of His grace, as here of His power in nature. HUPFELD renders Psalm xc. 2, as above: "*Bevor du gebarest Erde und Land.*" See his comment and note on *teholel*, iv. p. 6.

the idea of mighty forces in nature, of convulsive throes, of immense strugglings, of Titanic resistances, of a terrible ungovernableness in the chaotic and irrational material, as though rebelling against the Logos, the divine Word or Reason seeking to penetrate it with its formative, creating power, to infuse into it its spermatic ideas, and to throw over it the bridle and "the reign" of Law.

A similar feeling of vastness takes possession of us as we read Proverbs viii., 22–31, or the sublime description of the Hypostatic Wisdom, its eternal generation, its everlasting going forth in the ideal structure of the worlds. What a mountain of grandeur does it display as it so suddenly rises upon us from the comparatively lower plain of this ethical book! There is much of the same language we find in the XC. Psalm, whilst there still more vividly presents itself the thought of stages of antiquity going far back, one after the other, to that most ancient date of all when Wisdom was alone with God, the First Born πρὸ τῶν αἰώνων, before the beginning of His creative ways. We recognize in it the choral anthem of Genesis, with its key-note of ineffable times. There is the same thought of great successions, of an organic structure, like a κτίσις, a building, rising stage after stage to its completion. The Word and the architectonical Wisdom are one. It is not only the commanding, the fiat-giving voice, but the shaping, organizing, harmonizing agent, "rejoicing ever before Him, and whose delight was with the sons of men." Day after *day, yom, yom,* is he represented as contemplating this rising structure until its consummation in humanity, in the beings who were to bear His image, as He is the image of the invisible God, and whom He had "loved before the foundations of the world." The word day occurs here also; but were the passage read by itself, no one would ever think of twenty-four hours. The whole spirit of the language repels it.

The thoughts on which we have been dwelling, the ideas of succession, of generation, of struggle, of birth-travail, of strong resistance, are no less visible in the remarkable descriptions at the close of the Book of Job. As in the representations of the Psalmist the mountains and the earth are *born,* so here the sea has its natal period. There are more striking poetical accompaniments, but it is the same figure of birth, generation, genesis, φύσις, *natura,* which lies at the root of all early contemplative language, and, as before remarked, has become fixed, formed, fossilized, as it were, and unemotional, in philosophical and scientific speech. The sea issues from the womb of the great evolution; for to what else can the mighty figure refer? It is nursed like the infant; the araphel, the primeval darkness, is its swathing band. But it is an infant giant full of mighty energies. As it grows in strength, it becomes a most stubborn and rebellious power. It is well-nigh ungovernable. It even seems to tax the Almighty strength: "When I *broke over it* my law." There is immense force in the language as thus most literally rendered. Our version: "When I broke up for it its decreed place," comes near to it, but changes the figure, adding the idea of place to that of *law*, or *decree* clearly expressed by the word, as Jerem. xxxi. 35, "the laws of the moon and stars;" Job. xxxviii. 33, "the laws of the Heaven and the earth," and elsewhere, "the law of the rain." It falls short, too, of the significance of the preposition, עָלָיו, "upon" or "over it." The verb is a very common one, with a very uniform significance, but it sounds so strange here, that commentators have been far out of their way to get for it the sense of decision, which it never truly has, either in the Hebrew or in the Arabic. Umbreit shows great insensibility to the grandeur of the passage, when he attempts to get for it the sense of *measuring*. Schlottmann, the best of the commentators on Job, gives the true force of the word: "There is in this verb שָׂבַר," he says, "the idea of immense force." He finds in the passage the figure of "an almighty power opposing itself to the stubborn force of the young sea striving to extend itself towards the infinite." The poetry is in the reversal of the figure we should expect. It is law dashed, or dashing itself against the sea—the strongest mode of representing the ungovernable sea dashing itself against law, and reduced by it to the limits God has assigned. It has the same picture of struggle as is presented in the parturitive language of Psalm xc.;—an anthropopathism, indeed, but furnishing the strongest expressions for the fact of mighty forces in the early natures. It gives us most vividly the idea of a real law, a real causality, instead of a train of shadowy sequences such as a very late, as well as a very old, philosophy would represent nature as being.

The CIV. Psalm is full of similar ideas. The creative periods are evidently in the writer's mind, as is admitted by Hupfeld, one of the most rationalising commentators. Vast eventualities are there, but there is not the slenderest suggestion of their brevity, or of any solar day measurement. The impression is all the other way. Sublimity, vastness in time and space, successive stages of life, in the waters, in the earth, in the air—changes in the condition of the earth, the covering deep, "the mountains going up, the valleys going down," till they find "the places appointed for them." The soul swells with these vast conceptions, the canvas seems to dilate, but the narrow time idea nowhere appears; should it be forced into it, it would be like a collapsing of the whole picture. Its absence from such a painting can only be accounted for on the supposition that the writer of the Psalm derived no such thought from his inspiring model. Other passages might be examined in the same manner, and to the same purpose, but our present limits will not permit. My hearers will not misunderstand the ground or reason of this course of argument. It is not the absolute verity either of the Scriptural, or of any scientific view, as compared with each other, with which we are, in the first place, concerned. The beginnings, and processes of creation, in their interior causalities, are ineffable things. They are linked with the infinite, and must transcend the finite understanding. It is only shadows that we can see in the best representations of them as adapted to our minds. The Scriptural and the scientific may present a general outline parallelism, but it is no disparagement to the former to say that both will doubtless require supplementing, when we cease "to behold them as in a mirror enigmatically," or if we are ever brought face to face with these ἄρρητα, these now unutterable and inconceivable facts of time-transcending origin. In all that is here said, the design has simply been to meet that objection drawn from astronomy and geology, or the later knowledge of the cosmos, which I have unyieldingly kept in mind. It takes this shape: The view of things derived from the Scriptures is narrow; the creative account is rendered obsolete by the advance of science with its expansions of time and space. Now which is really the grander view? That is the question. Do the conceptions of the Bible, or those that may be legitimately drawn from it, *narrow* the mind; or do they, on the other hand, carry it to a height where induction falters, or utterly fails to follow? The question is not, which gives us the most of fact knowledge, or fact sequence, or of a dead mathematical science never getting beyond the bare facts of force and motion endlessly repeated, but which most vividly reveals to us, in its grand paintings, the true causality, the real law of life? Which presents the sublimer view, the correlation of forces, or the Scripture doctrine of the Logos? Let this be kept in view as the true issue and the true mode of stating it.

What, then, are the true ideas given to us in the First of Genesis as expressed in that old and peculiar language? They are: 1st, Creation, or the causing that to be which before was not, whether in so saying, regard be had to the idea, the essential form, or to the matter. 2d, Creation by God a personal and designing power. 3d, Creation by the Word, the Logos, or informing Reason, the Bible mode of representing what science would unmeaningly style creation by law, or rather evolution itself the law, however things may be evolved. 4th, Creation in time. 5th, An outline representation of creation in six principal times. 6th, Creation by successions, generations, births, or the bringing forth of one thing, or one state of things, out of another. 7th, Progressive creation, each step an advance on the one preceding, from the lower to the higher stages of being,—an idea which science has borrowed, but which her inductions cannot prove, though they often seem to contradict, 8th, The repeated declaration at each stage, ויהי כן, "and it was so," or it became *firm*, established, securing the permanent continuance of each new word, thus making a reality of that idea of law of which science talks so much, but for which, in her bare fact causality, she can find no real basis.

These are the essential ideas of the Scriptural account of creation. Science may worthily occupy herself with tracing and filling up, but can never reach, much less transcend them.

I have dwelt on this Mosaic account of creation, as it is called, because it has become the main target of modern scepticism. An affectation of contempt has been added to deadly hostility. It is too narrow, the time has gone by for any longer belief in it. The changes are rung in this way throughout our literary world. Ignorance is constantly reiterating it; the young mind especially is overcome by the sheer impudence of its repetition. But the objection is not confined to the creation narrative. The Bible, it is said, is narrow throughout. It is confined to the idea of one world in space, our little earth. It knows, moreover, but one world in time, the single earthly epoch, not long ago starting out of nothingness, with a blank undivided antepast eternity immediately preceding, then a narrow isthmus of time close shut in on the other side by a similar blank of undivided duration. In opposition to this I would present the greater time aspect of the Bible as revealed in its great æonic words, to which due attention has not been given by many commentators, as they have been entirely overlooked by the scientists, and the literary men, who are so fond of making these charges of narrowness. Let me have your patience in briefly dwelling upon them as the closing portion of this lecture. The Olamic words, as I would style them, have not only been too much overlooked in our Biblical study, but some of their most remarkable peculiarities have been covered up by general expressions in our modern translations. Of these, it may be said that none of them exhibit that startling force these words carry with them in their original Hebrew and Greek, and in the older versions, Greek, Latin, and Syriac. The reference is to what may be called the æonic words of Scripture, the terms of duration undefined by any ordinary chronological measurements, or used as transcending time altogether. One feature of this class of words, as distinguished from anything corresponding to them in modern speech, presents itself in their remarkable plural forms, so vivid in the original, but so disguised, in our translation, under the vague adjectives, eternal and everlasting. A necessity of human think ing brings into the Hebrew language, as in the other earliest tongues, a word for a time or times transcending history, and incommensurable by astronomical phenomena. It is in Hebrew the word עולם, rendered *age*, Greek αἰών, saeculum, aeon, and denoting a world, or world time, though sometimes hyperbolically applied to long historical periods. In its more essential sense, however, as used in the course of the Scriptural development, and especially in the New Testament, it means times transcending the historical earthly movement, whether regarded as known or unknown. With its plural עֹלָמִים especially, though so often disregarded in the translation, it brings before us the great times of the absolute kingdom of God; as in the XC. Psalm already quoted, where the divine existence is represented to be מֵעוֹלָם וְעַד עוֹלָם, from olam to olam, from world to world, as our brief earthly life is from year to year, or in its race aspect, from generation to generation. In Ps. cxlv. 13, its mighty plural is still further extended by a superlative word: מַלְכוּתְךָ מַלְכוּת כָּל עֹלָמִים, "Thy kingdom is a kingdom of all eternities," an olam made up of all olams, a world the complement of all worlds, a *magnus ordo* embracing all periods. It is this language which St. Paul had in mind, I Tim. ii. 17: βασιλευς των αιωνων, "King of the Aeons," King of the worlds, of the world-times, "Kinge of Worldis," as Wickliffe renders it from the Vulgate, *Rex Seculorum,* "*Malco deolme,* King of the worlds, or *leolam leolamolemin, for the world and for the world of worlds,* as it is given in the sonorous Syriac. Our version, "the King eternal," has a grand sound, but its vivid time significance is greatly marred in the neglect of the plural forms. In this way are described the "goings forth" of the Logos "from the days of eternity," Mic. v. 1. It has reference to the birth of Him who was to be "ruler in Israel," "ruler in the great kingdom of God," "King of the ages," though born in one of the least cities, of one of the smallest provinces, of one of the most diminutive space worlds of the cosmical universe. It was spoken of Him who by His personal union with the eternal life-giving, law-creating, order-evolving Logos, was to introduce a new evolution in humanity, raising it to a higher sphere transcending the physical, and to a brotherhood of higher beings which nature never could have reached, nor any scientific induction made known.

The word *olam*, and the corresponding New Testament αιων, are reduplicated and retriplicated to express the absolute eternity. They are employed to aid the human sense conceiving faculty in its goings forth towards that ineffable idea, which an abstract negative can only *name* in its unemotional barrenness. In the later Biblical Hebrew, and in the books intervening between the old Jewish and the New

Testament canon, olam is used for *world*, this world, the other world, the world to come, worlds in general, as expressive of the *malcuth kol olamim*, or kingdom of all worlds, according to the language, Ps. cxlv., xc., and other passages in the older Scripture, where the *world-sense* is disguised in the translation. The idea goes into the Greek of the later Scripture, modifying the classic αιων, employing its plural form, which is comparatively rare in classical usage, and giving it the world significance derived from the Hebrew, though occasionally found in the Greek poets. It is thus that in the New Testament αἰων, αἰῶνες, are so frequently used for worlds, time worlds, as distinguished from κόσμοι, or worlds in space— a plural that is never found in the sacred writings. The argument is wholly untenable that this word αἰῶνες, as thus used in the New Testament, denotes stellar or planetary worlds, or astronomical spheres in any sense. From its predominant usage, the Syriac translators mistook it in some few cases, and the cosmical view becomes still more apparent in the later Rabbinical; but it can easily be traced to certain crude scientific ideas that began to have influence upon this comparatively modern dialect. The expression, "*time-world*," may seem strange and forced, but the idea was very easy and natural to the early mind. It belongs more to the interior thought, and has less to do with any outward scheme of science, than the space conception. Hence it is less hindered in its goings forth by the limitations of our sense-knowledge. It has, moreover, a solid foundation in the necessities of the human thinking. A little reflection shows us, that the time of a thing is as inherent in its reality, or its true being, as the portion of space it occupies, or the force which may be said to constitute its dynamical entity.

For very clear proofs, or specimens, of this remarkable aeonic language, I would refer to such passages as 1 Cor. ii. 7, πρὸ τῶν αἰώνων, before the aeons, before the worlds, where the reference is unmistakably to ante-terrene, ante-mundane things: "The wisdom of God in a mystery"—"the hidden mystery ordained before the worlds"—the moral or spiritual kingdom, with its developments, existing before the physical worlds, and as the basis of their manifestation in time and space: βασιλεὺς τῶν αἰώνων, "king of the worlds," 1 Tim. i. 17, before referred to: Κατὰ πρόθεσιν τῶν αἰώνων, "the design of the worlds," Eph. iii. 2: "To Him be glory during all the generations of the world of the worlds," εἰς πάσας τὰς γενεὰς τοῦ αἰῶνος τῶν αἰώνων, the world that is made up of all worlds, all time successions, all the תּוֹלְדוֹת, or "generations of the heavens and the earth," all the evolutions of all the eternities. There is the language used in reference to the Logos, Heb. i. 3: "By whom He made the worlds, the aeons." Again, "By faith we understand that the αἰῶνας, the worlds, the world times, were set in order by the Word of God," the architectonical wisdom of Prov. viii. and Heb. xi. 3. "To God the Only Wise, be glory, and greatness, and might, and dominion, for all worlds of worlds," εἰς πάντας τοὺς αἰῶνας τῶν αἰώνων, Jude 25, Rev. vii. 12. "And He shall reign εἰς αἰῶνας τῶν αἰώνων, for ever and for evermore," through all the eternities of the eternities. We ask again: What are meiocene and pleiocene, and eocene; what are Prof. Thompson's interminable rows of idealess and conceptionless decimals; what are our millions and billions, and billions of billions; what are they all for emotional effect as compared with the living ideas that agitate us in the utterance of the ancient words, and their sublime reverberations? It is like the barren x y z of a frigid algebraic computation, as compared with the endless re-echoings of Handel's Hallelujah Chorus.

The power of this mighty Scripture language consists in the fact of its being so far above all earthly divisions, leaving them so far behind, not merely in numerical estimate, but in the power of thought they represent. In distinction from dead formulas, or dead facts, they are living ideas; they belong to God's great kingdom of life and spirit. They carry the soul with them to the contemplation of the greater chronology, the world of worlds, to which all physical worlds of space and time, all purely physical evolutions are wholly subordinate, and from connection with which, as I have said before,—but it cannot be too often repeated,—they derive all their value.

LECTURE V.

THE KINGDOM OF GOD; OR, THE GREATNESS OF THE BIBLE THEISM, AS COMPARED WITH THE PHYSICAL, SCIENTIFIC, AND PHILOSOPHICAL.

LECTURE V.

THE KINGDOM OF GOD; OR, THE GREATNESS OF THE BIBLE THEISM, AS COMPARED WITH THE PHYSICAL, SCIENTIFIC, AND PHILOSOPHICAL.

Preliminary ideas—Greatness relative—Distinction between *conception* and *idea*—Names of Deity in Genesis—Value of man not determined, increased or diminished, by any space extent of the universe—Psalm viii. and its interpretation as given in Heb. ii.—Psalm lxviii.—Christ's ascent above all worlds—His raising humanity to higher spheres of being—Beings higher than man—Bible presentation of these higher ranks of existences—Nature producing beings capable of interfering with nature herself—Science stops with man—Man, just evolved from a very low condition, the highest product of a past eternal evolution !—Inconsistency of this—The hideous *Hysteron proteron*—*Biblical order*—The Logos in the beginning—Idea first—The perfect first—*Physical order*—Matter and force first—The nebula in the beginning—All things made by the nebula—The highest in the lowest. Quantitative or dynamical, as distinguished from spiritual value: the first the ratio of force-being in anything to the amount of force-being in the universe; the second measured by nearness to God the centre of being—Faith, the value ascribed to it in the Scriptures as the measure of spiritual worth—Old Testament faith compared with heathen virtue—Dictum of Strauss that the Hebrews had the *personal*, the Greeks the *absolute* idea of Deity—Absurdity and falseness of this—The absoluteness infinity, timelessness of Deity, more powerfully and clearly expressed in the Bible than by Plato—Examples—The Divine ubiquity, Psalm cxxxix.—The Infinitely Near, as well as the Infinitely Far—The tremendous equilibrium as maintained in the Scriptures—Pantheism—The Scripture Pantheism, Acts xvii.—Anthropathism of the Bible—All revelation of the Infinite to the Finite necessarily anthropopathic: not a make-believe accommodation, but a real coming into the Finite—The Word, the Reason becoming flesh—Revelations through nature, anthropopathic—Scripture equilibrium of apparently opposing Divine attributes—God the Universal Power and at the same time a patrial Deity—No inconsistency—Boldness of the Bible writers—Philosophy cannot keep its balance here—Need of more study of the Bible as the great defence of faith.

THE greatness of an object of thought is wholly relative. So is the attendant conception: so is the emotion it inspires. It is this latter element that enters chiefly into the spiritual measure of value. In one sense, it may be said that we *are* what we *think*. In a still truer sense, we *are*, spiritually, what we *feel* in view of what we *think*. One soul may have a higher *feeling* of God's greatness, in connection with a very limited knowledge, than another whose scientific or notional views extend immensely beyond it. One soul may have a more religious emotion, a really greater emotion, a higher inspiration from the sight of a mountain, than another from the contemplation of the starry heavens, or the utmost thinkable spaces, and motions, and forces regarded simply in their mathematical interest. Thus, as has been already said, but will bear to be repeated, David, and Pythagoras, and Socrates, with their little astronomical knowledge, may have had a higher feeling, and, in this sense, a really higher view of that highest thing, the divine glory, as exhibited in the cosmos, than D'Alembert and La Place. The unscientific Jonathan Edwards may have felt more in the contemplation of the astronomical heavens than a Herschel or a Peirce.

In such estimates as these, a distinction must be made, too, between two words often confounded—a *conception** and an *idea*. In the same mind the one may be very small, quantitatively, and yet representative of an *idea* as lofty, as limitless, and as perfect as might exist in connection with the highest knowledge. Let me endeavor to make this plainer by an illustration: Abraham had very little of what may be called astronomical science. The sky over his head not very far off, and a great personal being ruling on earth, yet more specially dwelling in the vast unknown space that lay above the visible dome; this was his sense-conception when he thought of God, his diagram by which he represented Him in space, as he was compelled to do if he would think of Him at all. It was a very limited conception, we may say, but, after all, not greatly differing from the sense-conception we are now compelled to take when we would thus represent to ourselves that idea. It was, I say, his conceptual diagram, and ours is very much like it, though we know, as Abraham probably sus-

---

* The word *conception* is used, not as denoting a mere sense-image of God, but that sense-notion of His power, greatness, and other attributes, or that abstracted *concept* of His mode of existence, suggested by our best knowledge. The *idea* is different from this, as being wholly *intellectual*, wholly for the *reason*, and in that aspect, *perfect*, though *inconceivable*.

pected, that it was far from filling the measure either of the spiritual thought or the spiritual emotion. There is, however, no reason for doubting that the patriarch's *idea*, in distinction from the limited sense *imaging* his knowledge allowed, was as high, as complete, as perfect, in every way, as that of Sir William Hamilton. Above him and around him lay the infinite, as expressed in those three mighty Hebrew words that meet us so early in Genesis—those three infinities, אֵל עוֹלָם, God of eternity, אֵל שַׁדַּי, God Omnipotent, אֵל עֶלְיוֹן, God Most High—αἰώνιος, παντοκράτωρ, ὕψιστος—time, space, rank of being—living beyond all duration, strong above all might, high above every conceivable altitude of glory and dignity. What a contrast between this sublime monotheism, and the grotesque horribleness of the Assyrian and Babylonian theology, as deciphered from the exhumed tablets to which our attention has been lately called! And what must we think of the criticism that would regard these as furnishing the "Editio Princeps," whilst relegating Genesis to the position of an unauthentic, second-hand copy derived from such foul deformities! It was the same grand patriarchal idea expressed by Zophar, the Naamathite, Job xi. 7, under similar conceptual representations, and challenging comparison with any philosophical attempt to set forth the unknowable, whether made by a Spencer, a Mansell, or an Arnold:

> Eloah's secret, canst thou find it out?
> Or Shaddai's perfect way, canst thou explore?
> Higher than Heaven's height, what canst thou do?
> Deeper than Hades' depths, what canst thou know?

Heaven above, and the supposed Hadean deep below; these were the Hebrew conceptual limitations used to express the illimitable, as they were in our Saviour's day, and as they appear in His language concerning the doom of Capernaum. But the *idea* itself they are chosen to represent, has no sense bounds. The representative figure is, in truth, the necessarily finite diagram of infinity.

There is another thought on which I would briefly dwell here as introductory to the main argument of this lecture, though it has been alluded to in Lecture III. The enlarged modern knowledge, it is also said, has interfered with the old idea of Providence, whether as general or particular. We cannot believe in it, especially in the latter, as in former days. It is very difficult to hold now to any such minute supervision of human affairs as might have seemed credible for a smaller world. The immense size of the cosmos throws into insignificance the destinies both of nations and of individual men. The objection, moreover, assumes a philosophic air: it claims to be an enlarged view, far more grand and lofty than the old religious notion as grounded on what it calls the narrow space and time conceptions of the Bible. But with all its pretension, it is, indeed, a most human mode of thinking. It wholly overlooks the thought, of all others most important in a religious point of view, namely: that in the true idea of the Infinite One, there must enter also, as the complement of its fulness, the acknowledgment of the infinitely *near* as well as of the infinitely *far* and the infinitely *high*—a thought on which we would more fully dwell in a subsequent part of this lecture, as forming the marked distinction between the Biblical and the philosophic theism. We can think of but one thing at a time. He who transcends this, transcends it immeasurably. "As the heavens are high above the earth, so are my ways above your ways, my *thinking* above your *thinking*, saith the Lord." Vastness of space does not tire, innumerableness of objects does not perplex, their infinity does not exhaust: " Have ye not known? have ye not heard, that the everlasting God, the Creator of the earth,"—" He who sitteth *above* the orb of the world," עַל חוּג

הארץ — "fainteth not; He is never weary; there is no searching of His knowledge;" "He bringeth out His hosts by number; it is because He is strong that not one of them faileth." "How can God know?" Such is their real language. How can He be present in every part, with a knowledge of each thing, as it is, without losing for the time, the thought of others, or having His attention drawn from the great totality, the proper object of the infinite mind. This is simply a judgment of the infinite by the finite. We think of a great totality, or of a great system of causation, as something separate from its parts and sequences. We are *compelled* to take things piecemeal, as it were, not from the greatness, but the exceeding narrowness of our finite thinking. The idea of some all-embracing intelligence we take on trust as the necessary complement to our own deficiency. But with God, or a mind we call infinite, all effects must be seen in their causes, and therefore, as distinctly known, ever known, without any intermittings of knowledge, as the great movements, the great causes, or the great totality itself. It is astonishing how it can be supposed that this difficulty, which comes from the objectors' own poor thinking, can be remedied by that exceedingly human and finite idea of machinery, carrying on an original impulse like the turning of a crank, or the opening of a valve, and thus relieving the original power, and the original intelligence, from all after-supervision or control. A semi-conscious plastic nature created by God and endowed by Him with exquisite skill, such as Cudworth imagined, or Plato's Anima Mundi, which is very much the same conception, or a view, not obscurely intimated in the Scripture, of mighty superhuman beings carrying on the movements of God's providence; these have a spiritual dignity, though not unattended with difficulties; but the idea of a dead machinery such as we use—trusting all the time to a foreign force to carry it on for us—is wholly anthropopathic. It is thus indeed that machinery helps *us;* in ascribing it to the Deity we are measuring Him by ourselves, and all our talk of gravity, or of "the correlation of forces," fails to relieve the difficulty. And so we may say in regard to what is called a general intelligence. As applied to man, it is simply another term for imperfect knowledge; as predicated of Deity, it is without meaning. If the universe can do without God now, it could have so done without Him in the indefinite past. So, too, an absence of the divine thought at any time from any part is equivalent to a failure of that presence always and everywhere.*

But let us state the case more familiarly: For the sake of the argument, then, the supposition may be made, without objection, that the doctrine of providence, to the extent in which it appears in the Bible, is not incredible when connected with the thought of this being

---

* Instead of having any claim to be regarded as an enlarged or scientific mode of thinking, there is nothing, in fact, more deserving of the name of a vulgar prejudice than the disposition to limit the moral grandeur, either of a miracle, or of what is called a "particular providence," by the spatial or dynamical littleness of their physical means. The theist or theologian, of the Colenso stamp, may do this, but the man of science, however sceptical he may be, ought to know better than to reason in that way. He understands too well that the wonders of the microscope equal, if they do not exceed, those of the mere outline masses, or repetitions of masses, which the telescope brings to our view. His investigations are constantly leading him to suspect that the smallest things lie nearest the secret of life, and that the smallest movements, apparently, may be most closely connected with the highest workings of the organizations to which they belong. Especially is this belittling disposition shown, sometimes, in respect to certain miracles recorded in the Bible, and that without any regard to the grandeur of the moral reasons on which their true credibility so essentially rests. Thus the theologian above named objects to the miracle of the "plague of gnats" as recorded Exod. viii. 12, and referred to Ps. cv. 31. It is beneath the dignity of Deity, he thinks, to suppose Him immediately engaged in the production of such insignificant creatures as these Egyptian *kinnim*. Now, the language of the account

the only world, and the human race upon it the only class of rational beings aside from God and a few spiritual essences, called angels, dwelling in some adjacent spheres, atmospherical or aethereal, connected with the earth. On such a scale, then, we may regard it as admitted that the Scripture ideas of providence, of redemption, and the degree of divine care for men that they

---

is perfectly consistent with the idea of a purely physical process, if there were anything to be gained by such hypothesis. We know not what physical secrets may lie near the surface of nature, ready to manifest themselves suddenly when brought into the proper conditions; as new plants unexpectedly make their appearance in an old soil, or new insects, like our plague of grasshoppers, whose seeds or eggs may have lain buried for ages. But, as a miracle proper, what has reason to say against it, unless it can allege the absence of any higher law, or *moral reason* for it from the hyperphysical sphere? Beneath the dignity of Deity! But the *kinnim* are made somehow. Their *law*, therefore, their *idea*, their *reason*, must have had a spermatic place in the original plan of the cosmos. So the scientific theist must say, if he would shun the blankest atheism. But the immediate or supernatural production of such insignificant creatures! That is the objection. Let us look at it. Why is it more irrational than to have provided, billions of ages ago, for their ultimate evolution,—to have made a machine, to make a machine, to make a machine, and so on, to terminate at last in such a result? Where is the economy? Where the saving of labor or of dignity? Another element, moral and hyperphysical, the element on which we have so much insisted, is to be brought in to determine the rationale of either process, general or special, according to the higher laws and higher reasons of the great divine kingdom.

imply, would not be incredible, or beyond the very probable bounds of a rational belief. Now, suppose another world to be added to our knowledge, is this credibility diminished, and in the inverse ratio? Suppose two, three, more, to any extent; does the care, the providence, the supervision grow less in the same proportion: one-half as much for two worlds, one-third as much for three, one-thousandth part for a thousand? or does the moral ratio—the moral value—remain unchangeable, measured not by a varying universe according to a magnitude real or supposed, but by the relation, physical, moral, or spiritual, which each part, especially each rational part, bears to the immutable God? Does the measure of human sins, and the worth of the human soul, thus rise and fall? Bigger in a small world, less in a greater, vanishing to an infinitesimal in a universe supposed to be immeasurable? Or must we regard each individual world, and each individual rationality, as never falling below that estimate of moral and spiritual value it would have were it alone with God, the only world, the only rationality, in infinite space and infinite time? To think otherwise, as has been said before, is to suffer the lower power of imagination to cloud, for a time, the higher faculty of the reason; it is to imagine God to be just such a one as ourselves; it is to sink down to the low conclusion that moral ideas, truth, holiness, soul, Deity itself, are but quantitative or mathematical notions, having no absolute value, but measured on a sliding scale ever rising and falling with the space dimensions of a hypothetical universe.

The force of this pretentiously philosophic, but really anthropopathic view, is supposed to press most heavily on the scheme of religion called Evangelical, with its leading ideas of atonement and redemption.* The universe is too big for that. But there is no stopping here. Carry it farther, make the cosmos bigger still, and there must be a denial of any of that care for men which the easier scheme of "Liberal Christianity" is supposed to allow. Pull out the slide of the telescope, and a general providence goes with the particular; retribution, moral government of any kind, punishment of wrong by any designed process, penal or consequential, rewarding of virtue either by making it its own reward, or in any other way, become as incredible as special or general answers to prayer. Human virtues and human sins are small affairs, becoming smaller

---

* This is a train of thought pursued elsewhere in a note to the American edition of the Lange Commentary on Genesis, pp. 183, 184. It is introduced here, in an abridged form, as appropriate to our present subject. The paragraph devoted to it is deemed an essential part of the general argument.

and smaller with every widening of the physical scale. There is no holding on to anything partial, however large it may seem from our point of view. Imagine the universe larger still, and the generic begins to share in the diminution. Races as well as individuals disappear in the computation. Particular worlds become too small for the divine thought. Carry out the ratio, and systems, solar, stellar, nebular, vanish in like manner. We are left with a God who has no moral attributes, no care for parts of any kind, no thought of individuals, no knowledge, in fact, except of one vast boundless, indivisible totality. We have reached a region where all divine thought, all divine knowledge are merged in a mindless blank. The conception of totality, too, has vanished; for a real *whole*, in distinction from a mere *all*, or aggregate *mass*, cannot be truly thought without its parts. In our imperfect thinking, we may take it on trust from a higher mind without its filling up, or we may get an obscure hold of it from some dim and exceedingly partial deduction from a few parts, by which we leap the vast unknown, or supply its chasm by hypothesis. But to the Perfect Intelligence, where all things, if they appear at all, must appear as they really are, and in all their relations, whether universal or particular, there cannot be a *whole, as a whole*, without a distinct vision, and a distinct thought of every *part, as a part,* in its relation to such whole, and to every other part.

If, however, we admit an ideal change of ratio for man as accompanying a supposed enlargement of the universe, it will be in a direction the opposite of that which the objection seems to require. For all things that can be called *ends,* such as are all rationalities, all rational existences, whatever may be their physical proportion of being, such change, if admitted at all in an absolute estimate, must be in a ratio direct, instead of inverse. The anthropopathic view against which we are contending seems to say: Man becomes of less account,—it is less easy to believe him to be the subject of a particular providence, or of an intense divine care, as a member of an immense universe, than when regarded as dwelling on a lone planet, the only region of life to be found in all space. Reason teaches just the contrary. The importance of man as a rational being—his spiritual importance, though in itself an unchangeable quantity,—is relationally enhanced by the greatness, both spatial and numerical, of the rational spheres. He is the greater being the greater the city of which he is a citizen, and as embraced in a scheme of redemption designed to raise him to some higher πολιτευμα, some higher sphere. It is more easy to believe that for this the Eternal Logos became flesh, that now, through this great evolution accomplished in the Second Adam, man who had been of the earth earthy might be raised to a higher stage of being, and made "to sit ἐν τοῖς ἐπουρανίοις, in the heavenly places in Christ Jesus." Which things, says the Scriptures, "the angels bend down to look into." Thus viewed in its spiritual aspect, the scheme of redemption becomes grander, more gloriously credible with the expansion of the rational as distinguished from the physical universe. The interpretation which the author of the Epistle to the Hebrews gives to that wonderful VIII. Psalm, shows that the germ of this idea had, even then, its inspiration in the mind of the royal seer. This germinal thought was the destined human glory as shadowed in the physical inferiority itself: "Lord, what is man! When I survey the heavens, the work of thy fingers, the moon and the stars which thou hast ordained, what is man that thou rememberest him? What is a son of Adam that thou shouldst have regard to him?" It is then, as the Apostle interprets it, there comes the thought of a "Son of man," of "one made a little lower than the angels for the suffering of death, yet crowned with glory and honor." Dominion over nature had been given to man at his creation. But he had lost it, in its highest spiritual sense; for nature ruled over him. He was the slave of appetite and passion. David well knew that. But the "Son of Man," the typical humanity, was one in whom the language was to receive its highest inspiration. "All things," says the Apostle, in seeming contradiction to the Psalm, "all things were not yet put under him;" that is, under the Adamic man; "but we see Jesus," one in whom the dominion was to be complete; we see one man, the head of a new humanity, and "to whom all power"—the highest spiritual rule—"was given in Heaven and in earth." Such is the glorious harmony of Scripture. It is the same One who is spoken of in another Psalm, interpreted in like manner by the Apostle, as a conqueror, "ascending up on high, leading captivity captive," that he might receive "gifts for men," and introduce humanity itself into the highest spheres of being. Immense the rising, as immense had been the descent. "Now that he ascended, what is it but that he descended first into the lowest parts of the earth," κατώτερα μέρη τῆς γῆς, the lowest state of physical being, the silence, the darkness, the immobility of the grave. "He was crucified, dead and buried."

> Thence He arose ascending high,
> And showed our feet the way;

"above the heavens," ὑπερανω, "far above the heavens, far above the physical cosmos, to the spheres of supernatural and spiritual glory," or, as the Bible language gives it, "to the right hand of the Most High." "Lift up your heads, ye gates, and be ye lifted up, ye doors of eternity, that the King of Glory,"—ἀρχηγὸς τῆς ζωῆς, the "Prince-Leader of Life,"—"may enter in." It was that glorious ascension having to human sense its beginning here on earth, as His rising form faded away from the human eyes so rapturously gazing upon it from the summit of the Mount of Olives. We must not explain this away into a phantom show, or an unmeaning spirituality. The Scriptures more than intimate that this risen body of Christ transcended, in some way, the ordinary conditions of material being in respect to time and space. And yet it was a real cosmical transition, though to the questions, how, or where, or through what spaces, our best conceptions return no answer. It may have passed through all spheres, thus connecting man as saved and glorified, and raised above the physical, with the highest orders of being, and, through it, manifesting to them τὴν πολυποίκιλον σοφίαν τοῦ Θεοῦ, "the immensely diversified wisdom of God." Men may dispute the truth of such a doctrine, and deny its evidence, but they must not say that it carries with it a narrowing conception of God's cosmical kingdom. The very lowliness of man, physically, enhances the spiritual greatness of the Bible revelation. When science of herself can give us assurance of any such glorious human destiny, it may venture to challenge a comparison.

It is this idea of higher orders of being, of worlds transcending the physical, and of man's eventual connection with them, in which the Bible leaves behind it both science and philosophy. In the space aspect of the trine universe, as I have called it, the Bible language falls short of the modern scientific statement as numerically expressed, whilst excelling it, even here, in emotional power. In its time aspect, and time language, it has a conceptive grandeur, to say the least, which our decimal notation can never surpass. In the third dimension, or that of height, or rank of being, no scientific view of the cosmos comes near to it in spiritual elevation. I have already touched upon this dimension, to some degree, in treating of the two others. Worlds *beyond* worlds; that is the space view. Worlds *after* worlds, that is the time conception. Worlds *above* worlds: this is the thought to which the Scripture calls us; not in the space relation, where there is really no above and below, but in that of rank and spiritual value. Thus we speak, and truly speak without a figure, of the moral world, or the world of worlds viewed in the moral design, as distinct from the mere material evolution. Again, there are worlds, so called, and properly called, from the kind of beings embraced or the ideas manifested by them—worlds intellectual, ideal, artistic, it may be—worlds *ineffable*, transcending both sense and idea—such as " eye hath not seen, nor ear heard, nor the human heart conceived "—real worlds, yet having no reference to space, or correlation in space with other worlds, yet filled with a higher order of being— worlds hypercosmical, *supra-mundane*, if such expressions do not seem paradoxical; as where Christ says: " I came forth from the Father into the cosmos, and again I leave the cosmos and go to the Father."

There is nothing in science, indeed, to exclude such ideas of higher worlds than the physical and material, or of higher and higher orders of spiritual being; but this can be safely said, that since the days of Kepler and Newton, the course of scientific speculation has not been favorable to it. What is called " the Positive school," especially, with its many able advocates, is directly hostile to any such tendencies of thought. The reason for this, however, is moral rather than scientific. It comes from an aversion to the thought of anything superhuman. That would be too suggestive of the religious. Something higher than man! the conception must be barred out, or it will mount up to a higher, and higher, and higher still It cannot stop short of a highest, of a comparative supreme, some mighty personalty, having in his hand vast control of nature, though produced by nature, and thus falling infinitely below the true theistic idea of the eternal, the unoriginated, or the unborn. This thought of a physical Titanic god or demon, as a conceivable product of the great unknowable force, has already been dwelt upon in the First Lecture. Here would we apply it to the still more conceivable hypothesis of superhuman beings, simply regarded as transcending our own power of interference with the physical order. There is the possibility—according to the mathematical doctrine of time and chances, there is the strong probability—that this awful nature, from whose eternal play of atoms comes all that is or seems to be, may have produced such beings, immensely superior to man, and yet with no security drawn from any possible knowledge of nature herself, that they may not be beings of inconceivable malignity. Physical science has no *a priori* law or idea demanding that the atoms shall produce a good and benevolent, rather than an evil and a hating consciousness. It may be, too, a being or beings capable of interfering with Nature herself; as in the awful imagining of Milton :

> "Gnawing their mother's bowels ; when they list,
> To the womb returning,—hourly thus conceived,
> And hourly born, with sorrow infinite."

For according to the hypothesis against which we are contending, or the unqualified evolution scheme, nature has produced, in man, such a being capable of interfering with nature to a vast extent, of deflecting it from its course, or of making it do what, if left to itself, it would not have done. Now whether we call it the supernatural or not, there is nothing in the way of conceiving it as belonging to mightier beings evolved from this unknown fearful womb,—and to mightier still, and mightier still, as far as the utmost effort of our science-aiding imagination can carry the appalling idea. Thus science may have to admit the *miraculous*, or, not to dispute about names, the *mirabilia*, the things beyond our utmost sense, our utmost induction, stupendous wonders as judged by Hume's rule,

—in other words, phenomena depending on an unknown personal interfering will, far out of any traceable chain of impersonal physical sequences. It is these sense-transcending *mirabilia*, this thought of appalling personal interferences, which the infidel science would exclude from the cosmical being. But here they are again, in spite of "the Positive Philosophy" and on the very hypothesis that seems to exclude them. Here they are again, without the unoriginated I AM, the unborn God of Love and Reason, to shield us from their malignant power.

I have dwelt on this, digressively, to show that the very inconsistencies into which the system of unqualified evolution is compelled to run, in its denial of the higher being, prove the strong aversion of its adherents to the thought of any personalities above the human having been, as yet, evolved from nature, or that primal nebular substance in which all things have been lying potentially from the beginning. But be the cause what it may, the fact is undeniable. The scientific form of infidelity is inclined to stop with man. It would, perhaps, admit any amount of mere physical being as occupying the space universe; but rational being, if elsewhere existing, is essentially a repetition, in rank at least, whatever diversity there may be in form, of our earthly homo. Here they are the narrow thinkers; they are the ones who make earth the centre, or our own sphere of being the central sphere in dignity, if not the space centre of the universe.

How immensely does the Bible transcend this! How much more expanding as well as elevating its view! For here our discussion has reference mainly to this charge against the teachings of the Scriptures, that they narrow the mind, and that, in this respect, modern science has outgrown religious faith. The Bible does not, indeed, give us imaginative or descriptive detail, but it most vividly sets forth this altitude dimension of the universe, or of universal being. It transcends any view which would give it simply duration in time, or an endlessly expanding evolution in space—making it a mathematical universe, an immeasurable series of motions, a limitless play of correlated forces, an endless repetition of elemental phenomena—immense *length* and *breadth*, we may call it, with a lack of *height*, or an almost infinitesimal *thinness*, as compared with the idea germinant in all religious thought, and which the Christian Scriptures so wonderfully confirm and expand. The Bible, both Old and New, places God in the empyrean. He is described as "inhabiting the high and holy place," transcending in rank, immeasurably *separate* in moral purity; the heavens are not clean before Him. Φῶς οἰκῶν ἀπρόσιτον; He dwells in light unapproachable. His name is the Most High. He rules over the kingdom of all eternities, of all worlds, in time, in space, in rank of being. It is a spiritual as well as a physical kingdom—the latter subordinate to, and deriving its value from, the first. This kingdom contains countless ranks of being far below Deity, yet still many of them transcending man. The names given to them are not to enlarge our scientific insight, but simply to denote superlative excellence and power: Angels, Archangels, Seraphim, or burning ones, Kedoshim, or holy ones, Bene Elohim, Sons of God, Morning Stars, Thrones, Dominions, Principalities, and Powers. Immense the range, inconceivable the height in this upper direction. The more exalted their rank, the more occupied are they with the glory and adoration of their still infinitely transcending Maker:

> To Thee, Cherubim and Seraphim
> Continually do cry.

Again there are orders of being that may be conceived of as more nearly related to earth, and the lower physical being. There are references to cosmical powers of this kind of which science has nothing, and can have nothing, to say, either by way of proof or disproof. They are set forth in the Bible as God's ministers ruling in the elements, having an invisible elementary organization, yet exercising power over nature as man does; doing things which are not miraculous in *their* sphere, however they may be regarded in ours. The angels of the Egyptian plagues, the angel of the pestilence in Israel, the mighty power that smote the Assyrian host, belong to this class. They deal with the *interiora* of nature, the springs of nature, lying far down below our deepest science, the keenest search of our chemical analysis, the most penetrating gaze of our microscopes. On the pages of revelation the "curtain of the dark" is sometimes drawn aside, and these powers are symbolically exposed to view; but how often, in the history of the world, may be ascribed to such unseen agencies as these, events that so puzzle, as they are now puzzling, our best science! New diseases, sudden and strange in their form, ever and anon invade the world; inexplicable phenomena present themselves. Don't be afraid, is the cry; it is indeed hard to explain, if it be not jugglery and delusion; but even if real, it is still law; it is all law somewhere, and that comforts us, that magic word so much more tolerable than the idea of a near personal God, or the near presence of any of His more immediate ministers. All law doubtless, even as man's operations in nature may be said to be in accordance with natural processes on the nearer surface; but who or what wields the power of law in these deep interior stages, or these more hidden springs? Our scientific conventions take up the matter; they begin to trace some of the plainer sequences. They get hold of a few of the nearer links; and lo, another form appears, or some other inexplicable manifestations present themselves. All law doubtless, but how does that reiteration help the matter in cases where we stand in most pressing need of help, whilst medical science, and all science, instead of its usual vaunting, can only confess its incompetency? The same thought is suggested by what may be called seemingly abrupt transitions in nature—some revealed by geology, others occasionally presenting themselves in nearer historical manifestations. The clock strikes a new hour; we are startled for a moment; but soon comes the comfort again: there is a law for it somewhere; there are no leaps in nature. True, but what has made the connection? There may have been, as has been intimated in a former lecture, cogs and wheels far below where science sees; law has been going on in the silent approach of these in that awful depth, or there may be unseen powerful beings that by means of other natural forces have hastened the momentous contact. These may be ministers of God, or, take the pure evolution scheme, they may be of nature's own evolving, entering into the bowels of their parent, as has been said, or interfering with nature even as her younger child man has derived from her a power thus to interfere. The juxtaposition of atoms have made *our* consciousness, our thought, our will, our strength, our power to interfere with the all-breeding parent; why may not a congeries of higher and more ethereal atoms have somewhere and somehow produced a higher consciousness, a more energetic will, a mightier strength for analogous purposes, and still mightier and more science-baffling effects? I may refer here to the phenomena now predominant in what is called spiritualism, but which have manifested themselves in other ages and from the earliest times. The evidence has so accumulated, that the easy talk about the imagination and "unconscious cerebration," and the power of sympathy, has become stale. That there is a high measure of reality here can be no more doubted than some of the positions of science itself, as based on similar evidence. Equally clear to a sane religious mind is the proof that it is an evil as well as a very ancient thing. Its defenders adopt the common style; they, too, babble of "law," and show a like tendency to include all things in a godless physical system. In reference, however, to our present argument, there is need only to insist on the fact of its wholly baffling the positive irreligious science; and I would only remark, once for all, that when I seem to speak harshly of science anywhere in these lectures, I mean no other. Here, however, it is enough to maintain that no science can deny, any more than it can affirm, the possibility of aerial and aethereal existences, good or bad. There may be organizations transcending the utmost ken of the microscope or the laboratory, and yet as real as anything visible on earth—personal beings, benevolent or malignant, having control over the electric, magnetic, or odic forces, call them what you will, or themselves connected with them as correlated organic agencies. There is something very significant in the name the Scriptures give to some of these powers, whose existence it unhesitatingly assumes. It calls them κοσμοκράτορας τοῦ σκότους τοῦ αἰῶνος τούτου "the cosmical powers of the darkness of this world," aeon, or sphere—the unseen agents that rule in the dark world of nature, and who are also parties in the moral conflict in which the Christian is called to wrestle, Eph. vi. 12. In Eph. ii. 2, they are called ἐξουσίαι τοῦ ἀέρος, "the powers of the air," whether the term refers to the nearer surrounding atmosphere, or to the space-filling aether, a notion which the ancient mind, both philosophical and poetical, clearly recognized, and which modern science is rapidly confirming.

But turn we now to the higher regions of cosmical and spiritual being, and the higher beings before referred to as named by Paul in his glorious nomenclature, from whatever source derived: Angels, archangels, thrones, dominions, principalities, and powers. Immeasurable height! And yet above all these did Christ ascend when He "left the cosmos," and "returned to the Father, to the glory which he had with Him before the cosmos was." A narrow conception, shall we call it, this sublime scale of being, and that high destiny to which men are called through the mediation of the uncreated Logos! Place it in contrast with that well-known view of the positive philosophy which makes man the etré suprémé, the highest order of being the infinite evolution has yet reached after an antepast eternity of working. Not man redeemed by Christ, not civilized man, even, with all the animality and vice to which we give that name, but man as he was only a short time ago in the evolution chronology, when he first developed a thumb, and began to walk erect, though still a prognathian troglodyte surrounded by stone implements and gnawed bones—the Straussian or Hegelian man, in whom the universal force, the hitherto undeveloped cosmical soul, was just emerging into consciousness. Think of it! An endless evolution, an eternal working, an infinite causation, and yet an effect so finite. Nature has been working upward from eternity, and has just passed the long-armed ape who begat Prognathus, as Prognathus begat the troglodyte homo. What becomes of our doctrine of progress? As sure as mathematics, it should have been all evolved, all that we now have, over and over again,—all *out*, or far more of it *out* than has come out, incalculable ages ago. An eternal ante-past of progressive working! To what a height should it have arisen! It should have transcended all our ideals. The most exalted finite being should have been reached, the most exalted that our minds can conceive, instead of this creature man, so poor, so low; for my hearers will bear in mind that I am speaking of him as measured by no higher scale of value than that afforded by this physical hypothesis,- man evolved from nebular gas— man just coming out of darkness and so soon to return to darkness again—*e tenebris in tenebras*—man just stepping above the ape, or just emerging from the fungus, and having nothing to secure him against speedily returning to nothingness, or becoming manure to the fungus that succeeds.

This all comes from that hideous ὕστερον πρότερον, that inversion of all necessary thinking referred to in the quotation from Aristotle, Lect. Third. Nature first, it says, matter first, an impalpable nebulous nihilism first, the lowest and most imperfect first; life, thought, reason, idea, their junior products, and God, therefore, the last product, if there be a God at all, or anything to which such a name can possibly be given. And we are asked to adopt this, and call it grand, whilst rejecting as narrow and soul-contracting the Revelation which makes God first, reason first, idea first, the perfect first, — as has been said before—the imperfect and the finite ever a departure from it, whether in the scale of order or of time, whether as exhibited in processes of lapse and deterioration, or the contrary seeming of recovery and restoration in cyclical rounds. The two schemes have two entirely different modes of speech. Says the mere physical hypothesis: In the beginning was the nebula, and all things were in the nebula, and all things were self-evolved from the nebula —even life, thought, consciousness, idea, reason itself, having no other source. The other speaks to us in language like this: Ἐν ἀρχῃ ἦν ὁ Λόγος, "In the beginning was the Word," the Λογος, the Reason, "and the Word was with God, and the Word was God. All things came into being by Him. In Him was life," Ζωή, and "from this life"—not from motions, or molecules, or correlated forces, or the vibration of fibres, or the arrangements of nebular atoms, but from this life of the Logos, the eternal reason—"came the light of men"—the mind, reason, conscience of humanity,—even "the light that lighteth" every rational being, "coming into the comos." St. John and Herbert Spencer! This human light itself shall judge between them, and we need have no fears for the ultimate decision. But let us hear more of this magnificent style of language: "Who is the image of the unseen God, the First Born before all creation, the impress of His substance: because in Him were created all things,—things in the heavens, and things upon the earth, things seen, and things unseen,"—things of the sense world, and things transcending sense—all ranks of being, "whether they be thrones, or dominions, or principalities, or powers, —all things were by Him, and for Him, and in

Him all things consist, συνέστηκε, or stand together "—in Him the Logos, the reason, the idea, the wisdom, the eternal and "only begotten Son of God." This is the narrow view; this is the order of things we are asked to give up, that our minds may be enlarged by the more lofty method of science in its wholly hypothetical scheme of the universe,—a science which puts the nebula " in the beginning," and makes man, the ape-evolved man, the highest product that has yet been produced from a past eternity of progress.

There is a tendency, even among some who believe the Scriptures, to depopulate the vast interval between the human and the divine, leaving it an immeasurable blank, or a few angels, perhaps, who fly about the only inhabitants of the void. But this overlooks the sublime significance of the Bible language. The reason for it, however, easily suggests itself: The ascending view seems to impair the dignity of man as the subject of so great a redemption. But this is all changed when we come to regard that redemption itself as the lifting up of man into a higher sphere of being, and the rescuing him from that sinking into nature through which he tends to the level of all below, or to the lowest forms of a demonic animality.

The other idea proceeds, moreover, from a

false conception of dignity or moral worth. It confounds two totally different modes of estimating value, the spiritual and the physical—the quantitative or the dynamical, as compared with the estimate of faith, or nearness of relation in which the finite being, however small, physically, may stand to the infinite centre of all being. In the one aspect, the value of any individual part sinks in the proportion which its total capacity of being bears to the whole of physical existence. The universe, not God, is the sponsor and index of value. The bigger the universe, the less are human sins, the less the human worth. It is, as before intimated, a variable quantity, which, when this ratio is carried out, becomes an infinitesimal. When measured by the other scale, it is a *constant* quantity, unchangeable in itself, whilst, in this central faith relation, it may even be said that, instead of sinking, it truly rises, and that too in the *direct* ratio of the greatness of the universe considered as entering into the greatness of the Creator. In other words, the more glorious the universe in all the aspects mentioned, and especially in that of ascending ranks of being, the greater is man in this moral aspect, that is, when regarded as a rational, conscious participant and contemplator of this glory. "All things are yours; for ye are Christ's, and Christ is God's." If so be there are immense degrees above him, the higher is his own value as one rejoicing in it, and thus losing himself, as it were, in an adoring view of Him, *by* whom, and *through* whom, and *for* whom are all things. The lower the vale, physically, from which this rational, conscious contemplator looks up, the more beautiful and serene the heavens above, the more sublime the idea of the Supernal One sedentis eternitatem, "*inhabiting eternity*," "dwelling in the high and holy place, with Him also"—O immeasurable contrast!—with him also "who is humble and contrite in spirit, and who trem le h ..t my word."

Physical or quantitative value, as I have called it, is numerical or mathematical. It has a fixed summation in decimals, if we could find room in which to put them. It is quantitative, therefore, in distinction from that transcendental calculus which no arithmetical summing, no algebraic equation, no fluxional series can ever state. It is this moral nearness to God, as distinguished from such quantitative relation to the universe, which is so pathetically represented in the Scriptures. Man, as a rational being, is allied to the divine; the imaged likeness, though frightfully deformed, is still discernible to the all-seeing Eye; God recognizes this distant relationship as He sees him lying in spiritual ruin, and then, when he believes, the distance is gone; it is his faith which brings him near to the Infinite One, and makes him, in some sense, a partaker of His infinity. This is his value. Hence the power of that glorious scriptural anthropopathism: The Almighty Shepherd leaving the ninety and nine to seek the one that is lost in the wilderness. Hence it is that the ranks of ascending being, who are represented as standing before the face of our heavenly Father, rejoice over the sinner, the one sinner, that returns from his straying, and through faith in God becomes united to that higher fold, that higher spiritual sphere transcending all the spheres of force and nature.

In his mere physical aspect, man is, indeed, allied to the lowest things. Science, in tracing him through the inferior animal types, does not present this lowly aspect more emphatically than is done in the language of Abraham: "Who am but dust and ashes;" or in the moaning of Job, when he had lost his sense of the divine communion, the link that bound him to the Eternal, and having in itself "the power of an endless life": "I said to corruption, thou art my father; to the worm, thou art my mother and my sister." It is something more than a mere despairing ejaculation. In his physical being, "as of the earth earthy," man is, indeed, allied to all below, as in

Christ he becomes allied to all above. And this suggests the thought whether the lower creation may not rise with him in some proportional ascent? Scripture encourages the idea. The κτίσις, the creation, "the creature, groans with man." It is "waiting" in mute hopefulness, σὺν ἀποκαραδοκία, with bended head, with forward-gazing eye, with outstretched neck, as the pictorial word implies, with longing expectation, εἰς τὴν ἀποκάλυψιν τῶν υἱῶν τοῦ θεοῦ, "for the revelation of the sons of God." It is thus, too, we see what grandeur links itself with this human lowliness in the cheering language of the Prophet: "Fear not, thou *worm*, Jacob, for it is I who have redeemed thee; I hold thee by thy hand, I call thee by thy name; thou art mine." "Fear not; only believe." "For I am persuaded," says the rapt Apostle, "that neither death nor life, nor angels, nor principalities, nor powers, nor things present, nor things to come, nor height, nor depth, nor any thing created, shall be able to separate us from the love of God which is in Christ Jesus our Lord." What wondrous ideas are these! So new to the world! new to any phase of its speculative theosophy, newer still as a living emotional human utterance! "The love of God"—the love of God in Christ Jesus the Incarnate Redeemer—"the love of God that passeth knowledge!" That heavenly strain; whence came it? That superhuman flash of glory; from what philosophy, Greek, Latin, Egyptian, Chaldæan, Persian, Hindu, was it ever developed? All space, all time, all rank of being — the universe in its trine aspect — all is here. Science shrinks from the mighty declaration: " Nor height, nor depth," no power of the cosmos, either in its altitude or its profundity, can separate from God, or affect the estimate of souls that truly believe. Here, we say, is glory. But the infidel philosophy cannot see it. "Its eyes are holden." Extent in space, dynamical change, duration, motion, physical evolution, endless repetition of material being—these fill its range of vision. The height and depth of the spiritual universe, or as manifested in the glory of God; these are ideas which its inductions ever fail to reach.

So is it to a great extent in the literary world. The sublimest Bible truths are unknown. The organ for their discovery is not wholly lacking, but the frivolousness of the predominant sense-philosophy prevents their true appreciation. The mere litterateur sees nothing in passages which to the believer are full of glory, whilst things not worthy to be named in comparison from classic, Brahminic, or Confucian writings, call out rapturous expressions of admiration. The Bible is full of anthropomorphisms, they say. How offensive to their spiritual tastes are Hebrew gnats, whilst swallowing, without the least difficulty, the most monstrous of Hindu elephants and the most deformed of Assyrian camels! And yet to the devout student of the Scriptures, even the portions over which the careless worldly reader is most apt to stumble, are full of evidence that they are from an earth-transcending sphere of thought. Many have been thus stumbled, perhaps, on reading the glowing eulogy of the Old Testament believers as contained in the eleventh chapter of Hebrews,—or the long record of the men "*who pleased God*," because they had that thing "without which it is impossible to please Him," even their faith. They wonder that the writer should speak in this manner "of Gideon, and of Barak, of Jephthah, of Samuel, also, and of David." What was there in these uncultivated semi-barbarians that they should be pointed out as favorites of Deity, or as men "of whom the world was not worthy." To the Bible-taught soul the answer comes with an unearthly light and power: "They believed God," says the record; "they endured as seeing Him who is invisible." It is the trait which most allures the spiritual eye in those grand old patriarchal figures, so uncultivated, as some would say. In their unfaltering trust, they confessed themselves to be "strangers and pilgrims on the earth; they were looking for a better country, seeking for something stable, 'even a city which had foundations.'" They had that gem of faith shining far up in the highest heavens, and more precious in the sight of God, even when seen in the heart of an old Hebrew warrior, like Gideon or Jephthah, than all the philosophy of Plato, and all the pretentious ethics of an Epictetus, a Seneca, or an Antonine.

It was the saving faith of Samuel, of David, and those other rude old Hebrew men, so different from that which has been invented, and sometimes on the most untenable grounds, for what are called "heathen worthies." The belief in the salvation of Socrates, it has been said, stands on the same footing with our belief in that of Noah, Moses, David, or other Old Testament saints, so called, who died before the coming of Christ. But it is ignorance of the Bible alone that can confound the cases. The faith of these Old Testament men was ever a belief in a righteousness out of, and higher than, themselves. It was to this they clung, whatever the message, rite, or symbol by which it was represented. It was ever a righteousness of God's own providing. I will yield to no one in due reverence for Socrates.

But could I find that for which I have earnestly searched among his best utterances, any hearty confession of sin, any self-condemning humility aside from his frequent ironical disclaimer of knowledge, anything like the prayer of David or the Publican, any confession like that of Job, when, renouncing his own unsatisfying arguments, he falls upon his face and says, "I repent in dust and ashes,"—any language of deep self-distrust, any recognition, in short, of any the least need of a righteousness higher and holier than his own—could I discover any trace of these, I could draw from it more hope of his salvation, in Christ's sense of the word, than from all the fine sayings that have ever been truly or ignorantly ascribed to this noblest of the heathen, this prince of all the philosophers. "The heavens are not clean in Thy sight; Thou art of purer eyes than to look upon evil; Thou desirest truth in the hidden parts; O wash Thou me, and then shall I be clean; when Thou shalt judge me, then shall I be whiter than snow; a broken heart, O God, Thou wilt not reject; search me, O God, and try me; explore me, and see if there be any evil way in me, and lead me in the way everlasting; I will make mention of Thy righteousness, Thine only; for with Thee is the fountain of life, and in Thy light do we see light." When we can find anything like these utterances in Socrates, or Epictetus, in Seneca, in Antonine, in Confucius, in the Zend-avesta, or in the Vedas, then may we have some charitable respect for the parallels which certain literary men are so fond of drawing. Sublime examples for our argument are still more abundant in the New Testament, but, for obvious reasons, it was thought best here, and in citations to follow, to keep in view chiefly the earlier revelation.

"Against Thee, Thee only have I sinned." Hunt through all the dialogues of Plato, hunt through all the Vedas for anything like that. Sin as against God, against God alone; Socrates knew nothing of it. It is an idea hardly to be found in the classical Greek literature. The Grecian sage acknowledged a war in the soul; the lower had got above the upper. It was a civil war, destructive of all good. That he saw clearly. The disordered spirit he would compose and reconstruct, but he would do it by philosophy. He would make peace between the reason and the appetite. He would put to sleep the wild beasts, or chain them up, or set them in balancing antagonism one against the other. But he could not "cast them out." That could only be done by prayer, and fasting, and penitent confession that acknowledges sin to be in the centre of the soul, and seeks peace *there* by first seeking peace with God. It was the primal defect of the Platonic or Socratic thinking, that it made matter the original evil, and laid all our sins upon the wretched sympathising body. Of that older war between God and the spirit, of which the Scriptures are so full, Socrates knew nothing. The Psalmist, too, was acquainted with this strife between appetite and the reason; but he found not the cure in philosophy. "Unite my heart," he prays (Psalm lxxxvi.), *make one* my divided heart, as it literally reads, "to *fear thy name.*" How deeply Paul felt this inward strife we learn from that wondrous seventh chapter of Romans, and we know, too, his only remedy, "O wretched man, who shall deliver me? I thank God through Jesus Christ my Lord." "Let him lay hold of *my* strength that he may make peace with me, make peace with *me*," as the Prophet so tenderly repeats it.

"Our modern monotheistic conception of God," says Strauss, "has two sides, the absolute and the personal." "The first element," he proceeds to say, "is Greek,"—that is, we derive it from the Greeks; "the second comes from the Hebrew Christian sources." The distinction between the Greek and Hebrew conception, such a favorite with Strauss and others, is a mere tinsel antithesis, having a false show of learning, but without any real foundation. Especially is it false on the Hebrew side. The personal in Deity is indeed set forth in the Scriptures with awful distinctness, but in no writings is the absolute, the infinite, the unconditioned, the knowledge-surpassing, the time-and-space-transcending aspect of the divine character more sublimely presented: "The I AM THAT I AM, the '*O ΩN*, The *Being* pre-eminently, who IS and WAS, and IS TO COME, and whom no tense form can adequately describe—THE ONE—THE ALL—" who filleth all things," " who inhabits eternity," " of whom there is no similitude," with whom " one day is as a thousand years, and a thousand years as one day," whose " ways transcend our ways, and whose thinking is above our thinking, even as the heavens, the infinite heavens, are higher than the earth." Where do we find anything like this in Plato or Aristotle? For Strauss must have reference to the Greek philosophers rather than to the intensely personal conceptions of the poets. Where do we find anything in any of the Greek schools which so sets forth the absoluteness, the eternity, the infinity, the incomprehensibleness of the divine character? It does not detract from this, that such representations of the timeless absoluteness are sometimes made through the most vivid sense-picturings, though there are other cases, and equally sublime, where the general or abstract forms of speech are used.

It is so, also, in regard to conceptive power. This has already been alluded to in what was said of the old names in Genesis, and the comparison between the ancient and the modern sense-imaging accompanying those terms. God does not seem, after all, much higher to the modern astronomer than he did to Abraham. No figure of immutability surpasses that of the Hebrew שֹׁכֵן עַד, *inhabitans* eternitatem, " inhabiting eternity " — filling the changeless totality of being; or, as Boethius expresses it, *tota simul et interminabilis vitae possessio*. So also the representations of the divine unknowableness to which reference has already been made. Again, God's mighty harmonizing power—" the reign of law "—which he has established throughout the worlds, and the Scripture mode of expressing it, as set forth in Lecture Third. There is no show of philosophizing; no assuming to speak the language of any science. It may be said, perhaps, that there is an attempt here to get more out of this style of speaking than the words will warrant; but it cannot fail to be seen and felt how directly it carries the mind to the ultimate causal ideas, and causal forces, be they what they may.

Take again those attributes which, though physical in their manifestation, are connected with the moral aspect of the Divine,—the ideas of providence and omnipresence. How wonderfully are these brought together, in one picture, the near and the far, the intimate personality and the unconditioned absoluteness of Deity! We have a remarkable example in the CXXXIX. Psalm; the loftiest co ceptual expression of the space-filling presence followed immediately by language denoting the closest personal familiarity with the finite human soul: " Whither shall I go from Thy spirit, or w. ere shall I flee from Thy presence? If I ascend to the heavens, Thou art there; if I make my bed in Sheol, behold Thou art there; let me take the wings of the morning and dwell in the uttermost West; even there Thy hand shall guide me; Thy right hand shall hold me fast. If I say, let darkness bury me, the night shall be light about me. No darkness hides from Thee; the night shineth as the day; the darkness 's as the light." All philosophical and scientific language is ultimately grounded on figures; but what figures for the soul can telescope the *remote* more powerfully than these? And, then, in almost immediate sequence, the ineffable nearness: " For Thou dost possess my reins; Thou didst overshadow me in my mother's womb. How precious are Thy thoughts of me, O God, how great their sum! When I awake I am still with Thee." It is as though the soul that thus apprehends the Infinite by faith did, in some way, partake of God's ubiquity. In heaven above, in Hades deep below, in all conceivable spaces that lie between the remotest East, where morning begins its flight, and the uttermost parts of the boundless sea, the conceptual limit of the illimitable West,—wherever Thou art, there "am I still with Thee,—still with Thee —evermore with Thee." And so in the time aspect. God's eternal thought transcends duration and succession. The longest as well as the shortest intervals disappear before the timeless contemplation; as in the language already quoted from the Psalmist and the Apostle: "A thousand years;" it is numerically finite, even as one day or a watch in the night; but conceptually it is a symbol of eternity, of a timeless eternity. The thousand years represent the idea as well as the longest row of decimals. It is simply the most vivid way of setting forth the absolute timelessness of God's being except as He chooses to manifest Himself in the flow of the finite. Talk of the Greeks, and their superiority to the Hebrews in respect to this idea of the Divine absoluteness! what, as compared with the Psalmist's language, is Plato's labored effort in the Timaeus to give us the difference between αἰὼν, the immovable eternity, and χρόνος, or time, its revolving mirror. Indeed, the human mind must ever fail to grasp the idea of timelessness, but no language can carry our thought higher or farther in that direction than the solemn musing of this old XC. Psalm: "A thousand years in Thine eyes as yesterday when it is past, and as a watch in the night!" The wings of Plato's abstractions grow weary in every attempt to soar to such a height. Compare, too, the effort of the same philosopher to set before us his much-labored distinction between the τὰ ὄντα and the γιγνόμενα, the absolute and the flowing, the ὁρατὰ and the ἀόρατα, the visible and the invisible, the διοθητὰ and the νοητὰ, the sense world and the world of ideal or necessary truth. Great as that is, compare it all, I say, with that short soaring sentence of Paul, the *Hebrew of the Hebrews:* "For the things that *are seen* are temporal (πρόσκαιρα), they belong to time; the *things unseen* are eternal." Or go back to the older Hebrew prophet, the cotemporary and the minister of King Hezekiah: "Lift up your eyes to the heavens, and look upon the earth beneath; for the heavens shall dissolve like vapor, and the earth shall wear out like a garment; but MY SALVATION shall be for eternity, and MY RIGHTEOUSNESS (my moral kingdom) shall never fail." Take it in connection with the near language of the railing Rabshakeh, which now so repeats itself, in all its bald sameness, everywhere on the Assyrian tablets. What must we think of those who talk of these monuments as shedding light upon the Bible, or of the ideas it derives from them, or from the kindred Egyptian darkness. To a serious intelligence the conviction is irresistible that there was something unearthly in those Hebrew books, as distinguished from the literature of all cotemporaneous surrounding nations, and that this fact furnishes an unanswerable argument for their inspiration and unearthly origin.

And yet such is the nature of this vivid Hebrew style, that, whilst it rises beyond all philosophizing, the child can feel, and, in that feeling understand, its lofty meaning. It elevates the soul while it sets it pondering; calls out the contemplative spirit, showing the truth of that pregnant Scriptural declaration: "The entrance of Thy word giveth light." It quickens the intelligence through the awed emotion: "it giveth understanding to the simple." At the earliest dawning of the youthful intelligence should the grand Old

Testament ideas, and this sublime Old Testament language, be made as familiar to it as possible. It is, indeed, above them, but that is no reason for making it stand aside. Trust the power of God's word for lifting up the youngest minds to some good measure of its comprehension.

It is astonishing how ignorantly some of uor literary men will talk of the narrowness of the Old Testament, and the lowering conceptions it presents of Jehovah as an earthly and patrial Deity,—as a God bloody, vindictive, jealous, in the human sense, narrowly competing for earthly sacrifice and earthly homage—or pictured simply as thundering in the sky, or walking on the seeming vault above, or inhabiting temples built by human hands, or "snuffing," as the gross infidel says, the savor of the burning victim. Solomon's sublime prayer, before referred to, would be sufficient for the refutation of this, aside from all the other passages cited from the Prophets and the Pentateuch. Let it be remembered, too, how much that prayer reveals of the spiritual culture of the Jewish nation; Barbarians, as some would style them in comparison with the Greeks. In the simplicity of an adoring spirit, Solomon seems to feel that every heart in that great assembly throbbed in unison with his devout utterance: "Will the Most High dwell with men? Will

God indeed dwell upon the earth. Behold the heaven, yea the heaven of heavens, cannot contain Thee; how much less this house that I have builded," "*for the name* of the Lord God of Israel." Talk of the Greeks! Fancy such language used at the dedication of a heathen temple; fancy an Athenian, a Corinthian, or a Bœotian audience listening to such a strain; fancy the wonder that we should feel at finding a supplication like it in Pindar or Sophocles. How would the page be marked, had there been found in the writings of the noblest of the Greek theosophists, or the most celebrated of their lawgivers, thoughts so elevated, so unearthly, as are uttered by Moses, the man, as some say, who derived his best ideas from the dark animal-worshipping, or, at the utmost, symbol-adoring Egyptians: "Take heed lest ye forget the covenant of Jehovah your God, and make for Him the likeness of any similitude," as before quoted; "take heed lest ye lift up your eyes unto the heavens, and when ye see the sun, and the moon, and the stars, ye be tempted to worship them." Think what was all around this peculiar people, with their most peculiar literature. Think of this strange monotheistic cleft lying between a misty pantheism, filled with all monstrous shadows on the East, and the foul polytheism that everywhere spread beyond them in the West. What was the restraining power which so "dwelt in the tents of Shem, this Shekinah presence that abode so constantly in the ark of Israel." A due consideration of the spiritual wonder here, casts into the background the important, though still subordinate, question of physical miracles.

Strauss would regard the ideas of the infinite and the absolute as inconsistent with the personal character. But how do he and Spencer know what is inconsistent with the unknowable? Even pantheism may be so held as to admit the idea of personality. In fact, the only pantheism we need fear is that which strips God of His moral attributes by sinking Him into nature. I may believe in God as the τὸ πᾶν, and yet regard this Great Whole as a person who knows me a personal part, and thinks of me, and numbers every hair of my head. For personality is the most definable of ideas. It denotes a being, whether all or part, whether infinite or only very great, of whom I can use the personal pronouns, saying "He is," or "He is good," or "He is the rewarder of those who seek Him." Or it means one to whom I—even as a part—can say THOU —imploring Him in the language of the dying philosopher: O THOU Great ALL, *Summa rerum, Summa Omnium, Causa Causarum,* MISERERE MEI.

I can believe thus in God as the *TO ΠΑΝ*, and yet, if I am a Christian, can say, *Elohai*, MY GOD, —even as the Apostle warrants us, when he says: "All things are yours; for ye are Christ's, and Christ is God's." It was the Hebrew Paul that gave these philosophical Greeks a lesson in absolutism, when standing upon Mars hill he said: Ἐν αὐτῷ γὰρ ΖΩΜΕΝ, καὶ κινούμεθα, καὶ ΕΣΜΕΝ: "For in Him we LIVE and MOVE, and have our BEING"—not γινόμεθα, but ΕΣΜΕΝ: in Him we live and move and ARE.

The infinite can have its finite aspect. The infinite may enter into and act in the finite; may assume the finite. The denial of this is, in fact, the denial of the infinite. It is virtually saying that God cannot do all things; that because we cannot ascend to Him, therefore He cannot come down to us. It is the idea which makes intelligible, and renders so precious all the anthropopathisms of the Bible, as they are called. It is the ground of the doctrine of the incarnation. All revelation, whether in written language or through nature,. is necessarily anthropopathic. Those who talk of holding communication with God through His works use anthropopathic language. The Bible only goes beyond in making it mutual. God "comes down to see what the children of men are doing." The youngest Sabbath scholar is not deceived by the language; whilst the highest minds may thank Him for such a condescension to our poor thinking, our sense-bound conceptions, our yearning for communion in some way, between the infinite and the finite mind. We may bless God for such a mode of speech; but we should not forget how sublimely these same Scriptures set forth also the *far* aspect, the high aspect, the philosophic aspect, if any prefer the term, as well as the near presence. It is the great peculiarity of the Bible in distinction from all other writings, that it so unites the two—that with such unshrinking boldness it maintains this tremendous equilibrium of the near and the far, and sometimes in closest connection: "Am I a God at hand, saith the Lord, and not a God afar off? Can any hide himself in secret that I shall not see him? Do not I fill heaven and earth, saith the Lord?" But philosophy cannot keep its balance here. In soaring towards the infinite height, as it would esteem it, it loses sight of the infinite depth, the infinite lowliness; in stretching itself out towards the infinitely far, it fails to comprehend the infinitely near. The Scriptural writers have no misgiving in the use of such a style: "The high and holy One"—"the humble and broken spirit to whom He comes down." There is no incongruity; both notes belong alike to the mighty sweep of this infinite diapason. It represents the fulness of the divine, the fulness of Him that filleth all in all,—entering into the finiteness, knowing the knowledge, thinking the thought, feeling the feeling, and thus truly using the language of the human in its intensest and most human utterance. It is no inspiration of earth that dares to employ such a style as this.

There is a mode of intelligence which the Bible represents God as challenging to Himself, when he says: "My thinking is above your thinking as heaven is high above the earth." Timeless, spaceless, without succession, one great totality of cause and effect as they are mutually seen in each other; we try to talk here, but our words fail us. They are aiming at something; they are not altogether meaningless; we are confident that there is some reality to which they point, as we are sure that there is a real North to which the needle directs its tremulous motion in the dark night of storms; but that is as far as we can go. "Such knowledge is too high for us; it is wonderful; we cannot attain unto it." The Scriptures go beyond Hamilton, Mansell, and Spencer, in what it affirms respecting the divine unknowableness. But still it is the known of God that gives this idea of His unknowableness. "His thoughts are not as our thoughts." Most true indeed. But again the question returns, and we may defy any one to show that it is an irrational one: Is the belief in this transcendent thinking and knowing at war with that other belief on which all religion is grounded, that God may also, if it pleases Him, think as we think, and know as we know, and even feel as we feel,—entering not only into our finite thought, but into our sense-world,—yet remaining infinite, as He dwells unchangeably in the time-and-space-and-sense-transcending sphere? This is the great Bible idea, "the Logos, or Eternal Reason, becoming flesh." Believing it, we have no more trouble with the Scriptural anthropopathisms. To know, to think, comes under this term as much to remember, to feel, to love. We hail these modes of expression; we rejoice in them as the language of a father with his transcending intelligence coming down to his finite children, and that, too, not as a mere show, or make-believe, but as really entering into that lower sphere, and there really speaking the child's language as the truthful though far-distant reflection of His own eternal thought. All this, it may be said, involves the absurdity of the infinite becoming finite, or entering into the finite sphere without ceasing to be infinite. But how dare we thus apply our measurement to One we declare to be unknowable, and boast of the declaration as the highest attainment of a knowledge transcending the vulgar? If we resort to scholastic reasoning, it would certainly seem that the denial of the possibility of such a *becoming* would be a denial of the infinity itself, a limitation of the very idea expressed by the term. Another question is raised in respect to these anthropopathisms: Why could there not have been used a more philosophical style, though still human, or one more adapted to cultivated minds? The answer is, that whilst nothing would have been gained in point of significance, or any nearer approach to the ineffable idea, much would have been lost in power and vividness. All philosophic and scientific terms have sense images at their roots. It is impossible for human language to get out of this. It is ever metaphorical in the conveyance of ideas transcending sense. By the fading away of the metaphorical hue, words become dead abstractions, algebraic symbols, as it were, deficient in vividness of meaning, yet compromising the truth sometimes by cheating the soul into the notion that there is more in them than they really contain. When thus dead and dried, they are laid away in the fossil cabinets of philosophic, or scientific, or learned speech. They are the language of "culture," as Mathew Arnold would say. In this state they become a dead weight upon our thinking, whilst the simpler or earlier language, never losing its unchangeable freshness, leaves the soul at liberty to follow the illimitable idea, whether in the direction of the infinitely high, the infinitely far, or the infinitely near.

This same awful equilibrium, as we have called it, is preserved ever in the representation of the divine moral attributes. It is another peculiarity of our Holy Scripture in which no other resembles it. The terribly severe, the meltingly merciful; the inexorable judicial righteousness, the loving fatherhood; we find them both expressed, —and in the same passage, sometimes,—without the least shrinking from the near conjunction of things, to our thinking, so seemingly antagonistic. The same view may be taken of the unshrinking representation the Bible makes of God in His universality, as Lord of all worlds, "Lord of Hosts," of all transcending ranks of being, as מלך עלמים, "King of eternities," and at the same time, and sometimes in near connection, as a local deity, a patrial deity, a θεος πατρωιος, אל ישראל, EL ISRAEL, God of Israel, God of His people, —the I AM THAT I AM, the 'O ΩN, and in the next verse almost (Exod. iii. 13) "the God of the Fathers, God of Abraham, and Isaac, and Jacob," that much-used Old Testament formula in which our Saviour, in His argument with the blinded Sadducees, the broad churchmen, or *wide-thinking* people of His day, found so much of "the power of an endless life." It is that same presentation of the infinitely far and the infinitely near on which I have been insisting, and which is so striking a feature of the Bible as distinguished from all other books.

By such writers as Strauss this near patrial language, so precious to the believer, is cited to prove tnat the Bible represents Jehovah as ranking with the gods of the surrounding nations, like Zeus, or Thor, or Dagon, or Bel, or Chemosh. In such a charge there is wholly overlooked, or purposely ignored, these declarations of absoluteness and universality, sometimes in the same chapter, and so transcending the loftiest language of any philosophic or scientific theism. God is, indeed, set forth as a θεος πατρωιος, a patrial deity, the God of His people, of those who are near to Him by faith. Not unfrequently does this language become still closer, more familiar, more personal. He declares Himself a tribal and family divinity. "His mercy is unto children's children of those that fear Him." He is, moreover, the God of the individual, of every one who believeth. He permits the worshipper to address Him by those near personal pronouns that so astonish us by their boldness in the prayers of the Old Testament saints: "O God, *my* God; early will I seek Thee." "Why art thou cast down, O my soul; for still do I make confession unto Him, the salvation of my countenance"—my salvation ever before me—"and *my* God."

What the age demands is a more intense study of the Holy Scriptures, accompanied by the earnest prayer: "Open Thou mine eyes, that I may behold wondrous things out of THY law." The Bible itself must be brought out, and its mighty spiritual power unfolded, as the best answer to infidelity—the Bible subjectively, the Bible objectively, as the great standing miracle of human history,—as presenting a train of events most unaccountable in their bearing on the world's course, as containing ideas which no philosophy, no theory of development, can ever explain. To such study it will reveal itself as "the power of God." Other defences are, indeed, important, but without this they are shorn of the great strength which alone can make them available to the pulling down of "strongholds," and the overthrow of the truth's unwearying foes.

www.ingramcontent.com/pod-product-compliance
Lightning Source LLC
Chambersburg PA
CBHW031735230426
43669CB00007B/357